The ―――― UNICORN

The UNICORN

by Nancy Hathaway

AVENEL BOOKS
New York

Copyright ©1980 by Nancy Hathaway and Rosebud Books, Inc. All rights reserved.

This 1984 edition is published by Avenel Books, distributed by Crown Publishers, Inc., by arrangement with The Viking Press.

Manufactured in Japan

Library of Congress Cataloging in Publication Data

Hathaway, Nancy, 1946–
The unicorn.

Originally published: New York : Viking Press, 1980.
Bibliography: p.
1. Unicorns.   I. Title.
GR830.U6H37   1984   398.2'454   84-6190
ISBN: 0-517-449021
h g f e d c b a

Fourteenth-century Persian miniature illustrating the battle of Alexander and the one-horned beast.

Many people contributed to the making of this book. I would like to thank in particular Don Ackland, Dianne Burke, Thomas Burke of Pomegranate, Barbara Burn, Susan Chadwick, Gage Cogswell, Len Forman, Rick Frey, B.W.R. Jenkins of the Fowler Museum, Gene Kidwell of With Love, Roberta Kimmel, Laura LiPuma, Kenichi Otsuka and Kuzuteru Sudo of Kirin Beer (Tokyo), Diana Peterson, Ave Pildas, Pamela Prince of Portal Publications, Dominic Salvatore, Bernard Schleifer, and K. Yokoyama. I also want to express my deep appreciation to Annette Leddy, whose analytical and research abilities were invaluable.

Introduction   10

I   The Ancient Unicorn

The First Animal Named   28

The Eastern Beginnings   40

The Fierce Karkadann   52

The Unicorn-boy of India   64

II   The Medieval Unicorn

The Hunt of the Unicorn   76

The Lion and the Unicorn   88

The Unicorn, Wild People
and Wood Nymphs   100

The Magical Horn   112

III   The Progress of the Unicorn

Centuries of Search   126

The False Unicorn   140

Myth and Mass Culture   150

The Celestial Unicorn   168

Annotated Bibliography   186

For Bo

INTRODUCTION

Of all the legendary animals of art, folklore and literature, the unicorn is the one with the greatest hold on our imaginations. Other fabulous beasts — the griffin, the chimera, the centaur, the sphinx — are clearly inventions, existing only in a mythical landscape of our own collective creation. Based though they may be on some distortion of actual experience or some need of the human psyche, these other creatures immediately seem impossible, as incredible as dreams. But the unicorn strikes us as more than imaginary. It seems possible, even probable — a creature so likely that it ought to exist. And for centuries people believed that it did — elsewhere.

A solitary animal, the unicorn inhabits the distant edges of our mental geography. Reports of sightings have filtered back from many places, including India (in the fourth century B.C.), Persia, Abyssinia, Scandinavia, Poland, Florida, Canada, Maine, South Africa, Tibet. As a phenomenon, the unicorn has been curiously tenacious, with many educated people coming to its defense —

The unicorn in the Garden of Eden.
Detail from the painting Paradise
by Lucas Cranach the Elder (1472–1553).

not just as story but as zoological fact. Their theories have been numerous: perhaps the unicorn lived in the mysterious Himalayan Mountains, or in the Mountains of the Moon at the source of the Nile; perhaps the unicorn, like the pterodactyl, had once existed but was now extinct; or perhaps it was a mutant, an occasional freak of nature. Surely it did exist, if not here, in another land — if not now, in another time.

Other people, dull realists, have tried to explain the unicorn logically. It was based, they said, on the rhinoceros, a true one-horned beast, or on a profile view of an animal such as the bull or the African oryx. Their speculations have not diminished in the least the potency of the legend of the unicorn — a beast that may never have existed in actuality but which lives in some bright corner of the human mind.

The idea of a one-horned beast similar in many ways to observable animals, but better, was born in the inaccessible reaches of antiquity. The unicorn often figured in the legends of the East where, although described differently in different cultures, it was always a magical, extraordinary being. In China the unicorn, called the k'i-lin, was a gentle harbinger of good fortune and a symbol of longevity, while the Arabian unicorn, the karkadann, was a fierce fighter. In these countries and in others, myth and history were not necessarily separate. The unicorn was linked with Confucius and with Alexander the Great; the strength of its legend was such that, later, even Genghis Khan came into close contact with it. With the unicorn, fantasy and reality have achieved a well-balanced union.

From the East, the story of the unicorn spread to the West, where it was first described in the fourth century B.C. by Ctesias. A Greek physician at the court of Darius II in Persia, he had often listened as travelers told tales of distant lands. When he returned to Greece after seventeen years, he wrote a book about India, a place he had never seen but about which he had heard a great deal. A one-horned animal, he said, lived there. He described it this way:

There are in India certain wild asses which are as large as horses and even larger. Their bodies are white, their heads dark red, and their eyes dark blue. They have a horn in the middle of the forehead that is about a foot and a half in length. . . . The base of this horn, for some two hands'-breadth above the brow, is pure white; the upper part is sharp and of a vivid crimson; and the remainder, or middle portion, is black. Those who drink from these horns, made into drinking vessels, are not subject, they say, to convulsions or to the falling sickness. Indeed, they are immune even to poisons. . . . The animal is exceedingly swift and powerful, so that no creature, neither the horse nor any other, can overtake it.

Late fifteenth-century French border miniature.

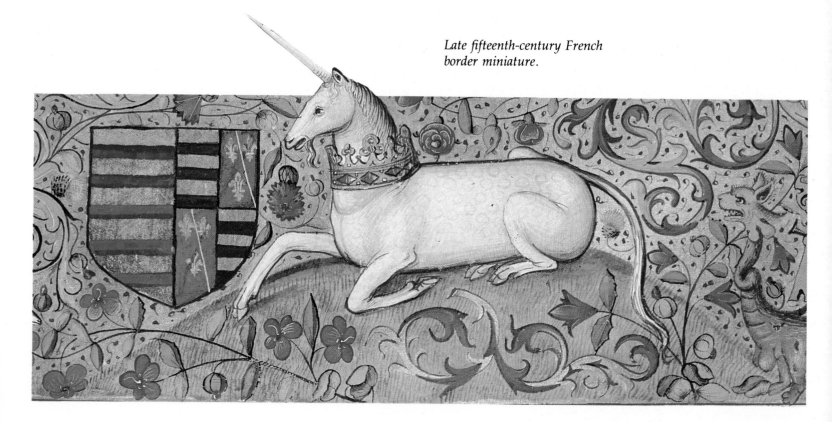

This passage, which became the source of much of the later legend, was widely read, and several other notable Greeks and Romans, including Aristotle, Julius Caesar, Aelian, and Pliny the Elder, clearly based their descriptions upon it. And so the unicorn entered Western culture.

Two other events, both literary, helped the unicorn on its journey. The first of these occurred in the third century B.C. when seventy-two Jewish scholars living in Alexandria translated the Bible from Hebrew into Greek. It is in their translation, known as the Septuagint, that the unicorn first entered the Bible. In seven different places in the Bible, they found mention of an animal called the re'em. No one was sure exactly what kind of an animal it was, although they knew from its descriptions that it was large, fierce and horned. Today, historians believe the re'em was a species of wild buffalo that, by the time of the translation, was already extinct in the Middle East. The scholars of the Septuagint resolved their confusion by deciding to use the term monoceros, later Latinized into unicornis. These references in the Bible in large part account for the entrance of the unicorn into European consciousness. Its presence in the Old Testament and, a few centuries later, in the Talmud, extended the unicorn's pedigree as far back as Adam and Eve. And because the animal was mentioned in the Bible, its existence could certainly not be doubted; the word of God attested to it.

The other literary event that secured the position of the unicorn was the compilation of a bestiary somewhere between the second and the fifth centuries A.D. by a person known only as the Physiologus — the naturalist. Over the centuries this book was translated into at least a dozen languages and copied over and over again, often with additions and alterations. Its popularity was immense, for not only did it present a great quantity of zoological information, all considered factual at the time, but it expounded upon the moral significance of that information.

Unlike the Biblical animal, the unicorn of the Physiologus was small but fierce — so ferocious, in fact, that it could be captured not by force but only by the lure of a virgin. Attracted by her purity, as well as by her scent, the unicorn would docilely lay its head upon her lap. Only then

Detail from St. Justine *by Moretto (1498–1555).*

The hunt of the unicorn is here presented in a specifically Christian context.

*Fourteenth-century French enamel. The
woman holds a mirror and the horn of the
unicorn. The hunter in the tree represents
the god of love.*

could the hunters take it. The complexity of this story, this connection between the unicorn and the virgin, gathers intensity with the knowledge that, very early on, the unicorn became a symbol for Christ. Saint Ambrose, bishop of Milan during the fourth century, asked rhetorically, "Who is this unicorn but the only begotten Son of God?" Saint Basil the Great explained: "Christ is the power of God, therefore He is called the unicorn on the ground that He has one horn, that is, one common power with the Father." In certain art of the Middle Ages the unicorn was even pictured as being held in the lap of the Virgin Mary in much the same way we might ordinarily expect to see the Christ Child portrayed with the Madonna. Nor is this linkage between Christ and the unicorn simply a forgotten concept of the Middle Ages. Even in this century, W.H. Auden used it in his poem "New Year Letter," which includes a series of images — the unicorn, the dove, the fish — all referring to the Trinity. He concludes by addressing Christ, the unicorn:

> O Unicorn among the cedars,
> To whom no magic charm can lead us,
> White childhood moving like a sigh
> Through the green woods unharmed in thy
> Sophisticated innocence,
> To call thy true love to the dance . . .

The Christian symbolism of the unicorn is a vital part of its history and has been much commented upon in writing and in art. Not only is it illustrated by the hunt of the unicorn and its capture by the virgin but also by the legend that the unicorn, merely by dipping its horn in water, is able to purify it, to rid it of the deadly venom of the serpent (Satan) so that the other animals — sinners all — can drink. Yet the parallel between the unicorn and Christ is a peculiar one, for if the unicorn is Christ, then the virgin must be Mary; her double role as the mother of Jesus and as the betrayer of the unicorn, is, to say the least, ambiguous. The reason for this confusion of analogy may lie in the varied nature of the unicorn itself, for it contains a multiplicity of meanings.

Because the unicorn was associated with the virgin it became a symbol for chastity. Representations of this theme in paintings, miniatures and tapestries of the Middle Ages and Renaissance often show a pair of unicorns pulling a carriage

Mid-fifteenth-century Florentine miniature illustrating Petrarch's The Triumph of Chastity, *a poem inspired by his unconsummated love for Laura. This image of a victory chariot drawn by unicorns was popular during the late Middle Ages.*

upon which a young woman is riding. This particular motif, called the "Triumph of Chastity," illustrated a poem written by Petrarch in the fourteenth century mourning the loss of his beloved Laura. In other variations on the same theme, a young woman and a unicorn are shown in allegorical battle against the forces of lust and immodesty. The unicorn's prominence in these pieces of art varies: sometimes the woman fighting on the side of chastity is riding a unicorn, while in other works the unicorn appears only as a tiny figure in her banner. (The opposition, also a woman, is frequently shown riding a bear.) In either situation, the presence of the unicorn is a clear indication of the virtue under consideration. Just as the unicorn represented the virtues of women, it also stood for the valor and nobility of men — and knights in particular. It was frequent-

ly used in heraldry, for it implied the twin virtues of strength and purity — might and right.

Even as the unicorn symbolizes chastity, it also has strong erotic connotations, which are present in both the literature and the artwork of the period. In much of the art, religious references have been completely eliminated, so that all that remains is the unicorn, tamed in a woman's lap. Sometimes the connection with chastity is still evident, as indicated by the mood of the painting, the demeanor of the woman, or perhaps the title. But at other times, in other pieces of art, the woman looks quite alluring, and occasionally she is completely naked. In these works the unicorn represents the lover, trapped and seduced by his beloved.

The poet Thibaut, count of Champagne and Brie and king of Navarre, was a religious tyrant

Late fifteenth-century Swiss tapestry. The unicorn shields the maiden from lustful love. "He who hunts for sensual pleasure will find grief," she admonishes. The huntsman protests, "I hunt for faithfulness."

who once ordered and watched the burning to death of one hundred eighty-three people convicted of being heretics. He was also one of the best-loved songwriters of the thirteenth century, and it is primarily for this that he is remembered. One of his verses depicts the relationship between the unicorn and the lover:

> The unicorn and I are one:
> He also pauses in amaze
> Before some maiden's magic gaze,
> And while he wonders, is undone.
> On some dear breast he slumbers deep
> And Treason slays him in that sleep.
> Just so have ended my Life's days;
> So Love and my Lady lay me low.
> My heart will not survive this blow.

The more libidinous implications of the unicorn are further illustrated by its association with the wild people. The wild people were a strange conception (or projection) of the people of the Middle Ages. They were savages who lived, it was said, deep in the forests, naked but covered with hair. While ordinary men could not tame or capture the one-horned beast, the wild people fought the unicorn fearlessly and could ride upon its back. Wild women in particular are often shown riding the unicorn; they are always naked, with streaming hair. The impact of these portrayals is definitely erotic.

No one dealt with the sexual implications of the unicorn with greater ribaldry and insight than François Rabelais, the sixteenth-century writer and physician. In *Pantagruel* he wrote of a journey to the land of Satin, where everything is made of Tapestry:

I saw there two and thirty unicorns. They are a cursed sort of creature much resembling a fine horse, unless it be that their heads are like a stag's, their feet like an elephant's, their tails like a white boar's, and out of each of their foreheads sprouts a sharp black horn, some six or seven feet long; commonly, it dangles down like a turkey-cock's comb. When the unicorn has a mind to fight, or put it to any other use, what does he do but make it stand, and then it is as straight as the arrow.

Diane de Poitiers, *powerful mistress of Henry II of France, by Francois Clouet (1522–1572). The unicorn appears on a chairback tapestry in the background (see detail).*

Nor does that complete the catalogue of symbols. In a twelfth-century rulebook for nuns, the unicorn is described as wicked, wrathful, an emblem for violent people. Three hundred years later Albrecht Dürer, in his engraving *The Rape of Persephone,* pictures Pluto, the god of the underworld, grabbing the naked Persephone and preparing to carry her away to his dark world. His mount is a unicorn. And so the unicorn — symbol of earthly and heavenly love — also signifies death and violence. In addition, the unicorn had alchemical meanings and was linked with the philosophical implications of mercury. It has represented solitude, the monastic life, the moon, and even, according to one commentator, sodomy.

The unicorn's significance was not, however, merely symbolic. Just as the creature represented religious and sexual purity, so it came to be thought of as a means to physical purity, or health. The unicorn was believed to have many practical applications for humanity, most of which revolved about its magical horn. These legends, which arose out of the unicorn's ability to purify poisioned water, attributed to the horn the abilities to detect poison, to cure impotent men and barren women of their afflictions, and to prevent plague, epilepsy and a host of other diseases. The horn

OPPOSITE
The Rape of Persephone, *steel engraving by Albrecht Dürer (1471–1528). Pluto rides a unicorn, symbolizing death and destruction.*

The Vice of Intemperance *is illustrated by the unicorn's dalliance with the virgin, which always results in its capture.*

Marginal decoration from the Ormesby Psalter, early fourteenth century.

was a priceless commodity, and many doctors and patients of the day swore by its efficacy in curing nearly any undesirable condition. There were doubters, however; in the sixteenth century Ambroise Paré, the great French surgeon, announced that the virtues of unicorn horn might be fewer than commonly thought. "Physicians are frequently compelled to prescribe unicorn or rather to allow patients to have them because they demand such remedies," he said. "For if it happened that a patient who had made such a re-

Detail from fifteenth-century German fresco. The hunt of the unicorn was also interpreted as the story of Christ, who here rides the unicorn.

quest were to die without receiving what he wanted, the family would expel such physicians and disparage them in gossip as 'quite out of touch.' " Paré's strong public statements against the horn did little to abate the demand for it, though he was not alone in his assessment of its value. By that time belief in the unicorn had started to diminish; nonetheless, demand for the horn was still strong, and pharmacies throughout Europe carried powders and chunks of horn said to be unicorn. In England it was not until 1746

Detail from
Jean Duvet engraving

Miniature from the Stuttgart Psalter, dated about 820. The unicorn, mentioned several times in the Septuagint translation of the Old Testament, also became associated with Jesus Christ as a symbol of purity.

that official recognition of the horn as an effective medication was withdrawn.

The history of the unicorn, then, is complex and varied, caught up with the concepts of purity, sexuality, magical power, strength, suffering, and death. The ideas behind the unicorn have often been hidden in the shadows of time and conjecture, but the image of the unicorn, which has been with us since antiquity, is remarkably clear. Today, after a gradual decline in interest, the unicorn is experiencing a renaissance. Unfortunately, it has often been made bland, its force diluted by sentimentality and whimsy.

The original image and spirit of the unicorn are the concerns of this book. It presents lore and legends from various times and cultures. Many of the stories have been expanded considerably, but all (except the last) are derived from history: from an ancient tale, from a story implied in a piece of artwork or literature, or from the life of a historical figure (such as James I of England) who is in some way connected with the unicorn. Like other resonant fictions, the myth of the unicorn enriches our lives and can tell us much about ourselves and our aspirations. It exists on its own — beyond interpretation.

This book, then, is not a contemporary fantasy. (An excellent one, Peter S. Beagle's *The Last Unicorn*, already exists.) Nor is it an analysis of the history of the legend (for that, read *The Lore of the Unicorn* by Odell Shepard) or a discussion of the artwork (a subject dealt with in Margaret B. Freeman's *The Unicorn Tapestries*). Instead, this book presents the stories themselves, drawn from the historical record and transformed — sometimes in small ways, sometimes in large — to create a series of visions of that wondrous being, the living unicorn.

Fifteenth-century Italian painting, probably from a marriage chest, illustrating Chastity enthroned. At her side are Diana, goddess of the hunt, and the unicorn.

PART ONE
THE
ANCIENT UNICORN

I

THE FIRST ANIMAL NAMED

When God created the earth, he made a river which flowed from the Garden of Eden over braided veins of onyx and gold. The river split into four branches: one was called the Pison, one was the Euphrates, one flowed east toward Assyria, and one circled Ethiopia. Everywhere the rivers ran, the land was filled with living things. There were vines, spiky yucca and dry-dropping quince, mosses, papyrus reeds and citrus. And there were creatures. They all were beautiful. But only two of them had names—Adam and Eve, who did not realize that they had dominion over the others.

Then God told Adam to name the animals. All the creatures gathered around: those that crawled and those that flew and those that swam in the rivers; creatures with four legs and creatures with two, those with bushy tails and those who could see in the dark. They were all equal, and Adam had always been one of them. Yet as he began to name them, he drew himself apart. And the first animal he named was the unicorn.

The Creation of the Birds and Animals, *from the Holkham Bible.*

The unicorn with Adam and Eve in the Garden of Eden, from Johann Joachim Becher's Illustratus Medicinalis, *1663.*

Detail from Creation tapestry.

When the Lord heard the name Adam had spoken, he reached down and touched the tip of the single horn growing from the animal's forehead. From that moment on, the unicorn was elevated above other beasts.

Adam and Eve rode upon the unicorn's back through the winding pathways of the garden, and all of creation lived in peace until Adam and Eve became curious about that which had been forbidden. Then they tasted the fruit of the tree of knowledge and, ashamed, they clothed themselves with woven leaves. When God saw what they had done, he drove them from the Garden of Eden and barred the entrance with cherubs who waved flaming swords. But the Lord gave the unicorn the choice of remaining in paradise or accompanying Adam and Eve out into the world, where there was pestilence and war, and pain in childbirth and in death. The unicorn looked to the angels hovering above the gate with their burning swords, and looked to Adam and Eve—and followed them. Forever after the unicorn was blessed for its compassion, for it could have stayed in that place of ideal beauty and delight, but instead, out of love, it chose the hard way—the human way.

Daniel lived his life in captivity, a soothsayer for kings. From the time he was brought to Nebuchadnezzar as a child, he saw visions at night. He knew secrets, could read the future in the throw of the stones, and understood the significance of numbers. It was in Sushan, as he was sleeping on the ground, that Daniel first saw the unicorn.

At that time, Daniel was worried; his visions chased him all night long, and for many months he had not been still in his mind. For once, he would have liked a night to pass without event, without shimmering edges. This night, the winds blew around him, and he buried his face in his sleeves. Eventually he fell asleep, but once again his sleep was troubled. In his dream he was at the River Ulai. By its bank stood a ram with two horns, one larger than the other. The ram was growing; it expanded with every breath, and its gray sides looked like smooth brains. With every breath, it grew to the west, and the north, and the south. It was invincible.

Then the unicorn appeared. It looked like a goat, bearded, with quick forelegs and a single horn. It stood above the curve of the river, and its eyes were white and red with rage. With lowered horn it stalked across the river toward the ram. With its every footstep ripples swelled outward and broke against the banks like tidal waves. The wind whipped around its horn and sounded low, like thunder, like the call of whales; and lightning splintered from the tip of its horn.

The unicorn pursued the ram until the two animals were facing each other. The ram backed up, the unicorn pushed forward. Finally the two beasts stood still. They both lowered their horns and

Detail from Creation tapestry, eleventh or twelfth century. In right segment, Adam is naming the animals.

stamped upon the ground with their hoofs. The unicorn lunged at the ram's head; with a swoop of its sword-like horn, it severed the horns of the ram, knocked the beast into the river and trampled it. The muddy waters of the Ulai swirled scarlet.

Then the unicorn began to grow. Its single horn, now tipped with blood, broke off, and in its place there sprung up four smaller horns. Out of one of them sprouted yet another, which grew greater than the others until it touched the heavens. Stars plummeted in a veil of sparks and the ground was covered with the dust of comets.

Daniel knew not what the dream meant, and he was faint with confusion and worry. Searching for meaning, he dipped his fingers in the river and touched the cast-off horn of the unicorn. At once, he heard a voice from between the banks of the Ulai that made the earth beneath him vibrate. He whirled around, and saw before him the Angel Gabriel, with wings like rainbows.

Gabriel told him what the vision meant. The ram's two horns were the kings of Media and Persia—and although one king was greater than the other, they lived together side by side. But then the rough unicorn with its one horn approached; the horn was Alexander, the ruler of Greece, who one day would conquer the other kingdoms with his sword. But his kingdom, great as it would be, would not last. Four kings without his power would rise up when he died and divide his kingdom among them. One kingdom would become four, and out of one of those would come Antiochus Epiphanes, who would persecute the Jews and defile the temple.

That night, Daniel became sick and all the next day was nauseous and could not eat. Nonetheless, he went about his daily tasks and was relieved when, the next night, his sleep was cloudy and unremarkable. Daniel told his vision to the king. And in time the events he had prophesied came to pass.

The Creation of the Animals
by Raphael (1483–1520).

Miniature in early fifteenth-century manuscript by Bartholomaeus Anglicus. The unicorn and other animals watch as God joins Adam and Eve together.

David was the youngest of eight sons. For many years his father Jesse sent him out to tend the sheep. During this time, he wandered about the valley, learning its secrets; he learned how shadows fell at dusk, and lengthened and disappeared, and he learned about the growing of the grasses, and how the sounds of wind and sheep and bees and calling birds could grow together into a single chord. He played his harp and made up many songs, and although his songs were laughed at by his brothers David was undeterred, and music flowed out of him every time his fingers strummed the taut strings of his harp.

One day, when David went out to watch the

sheep, he felt angry and more than once he smashed his staff against the side of a tree. He had fought that morning with his older brothers Eliab and Abinadab because he did not want to tend the sheep any longer. Each of the elder brothers had, in his turn, herded the flocks, but as soon as the next brother reached a certain age, the task went to him and the older brother was freed for more interesting pursuits. But for David there was no younger brother; he was the last one. The brothers laughed. They had little love for David, and at the same time they remembered their own sheep-herding days with some fondness, for none of them had prospered in his heart since putting down the shepherd's staff. David pleaded with his brothers and with his father. He wanted nothing more than to leave the sheep behind and study music, to learn the psaltery, to hear the trumpet, to fashion bells and cymbals and to listen to the great musicians. His family, however, would have none of it, and they mocked his ambitions.

And so, that day, David was bitter, and although the strings of the harp sounded as pure as ever, no words came, and he plucked the strings aimlessly.

In the Bible, the unicorn is a symbol of strength. This miniature, completed about 970 in a Spanish abbey, illustrates Daniel's prophetic dream.

He thought that if he could run up and down the hills or swim in the seas he might feel better. Instead, he contented himself with what little exploring he could do. When he saw a mountain he could not recall having seen before, he herded the flock up to the top of it and set them grazing there. At the top of the mountain, he felt calmer and began to beat a gentle rhythm with his hand upon his knee. He was almost ready to burst into song when the earth trembled and the sheep stood still; the mountain heaved up into the clouds and the air shuddered.

David saw that the mountain he had climbed with his sheep was not a mountain at all but a giant unicorn. He was standing upon its broad back. In front of him rose its stupendous neck. The unicorn was shaking its head and stamping its foot, and its mane flowed like streams of lava. At the top of its head, David saw the horn, of ivory and gold, ascending to the clouds. He grabbed hold of the mane, braced his feet against the unicorn's thick neck, and began to climb. It was hard work, and by the time David reached the top of the great head sweat was dripping from his brow and his heart was pounding loudly. When he reached the horn he saw that it was like a ladder, and he climbed up it until he reached heaven. He felt a silent ringing in the air and then, from every direction, came a sound—a clear, low note that made waves in the air as slow and strong as waves in the ocean. Each wave crashed against him, and the waves kept coming and coming although the sound had been uttered only one time. Then David heard the note again. Every part of his body vibrated in tune with the sound. He knew it was the name of God, and he was afraid.

Adam Naming the Animals, *illustration in a Dutch Bible about 1440.*

"Let me down," he begged. "If you let me down, I will tend the sheep forever and never complain. And I'll build you a temple as big as the horn of the unicorn." The Lord listened to his request, and to the musical quality of his voice. And he sent down a lion.

The unicorn fears no other animal although there are many it disdains. But it respects the lion, and so the unicorn knelt on the ground. Seeing his chance, David climbed off the horn, grabbed the mane with his blistered hands and slid down the neck. He herded his sheep down the unicorn's wide flanks back to the valley where they were accustomed to graze. When he turned around the unicorn had disappeared. But the lion was still there, moving heavily toward him. Slowly it began to gallop and then it roared, a long guttural sound. When David saw its teeth, like a mouthful of dag-gers, he sang this song:

Be not thou far from me, O Lord:
Deliver my soul from the sword;
My darling from the power of the dog.
Save me from the lion's mouth;
For thou hast heard me from the horns of the
    unicorns.

The lion heard the song; his movements became slower and slower as he reached the spot where the young shepherd stood. And then, while David trembled, the lion knelt.

Generations passed. The earth became a corrupt and violent place. The joy of creation had grown sour and God wanted to destroy the earth and begin anew. He spoke to Noah, whose family alone among all of humanity he deemed worth saving, and told him to build an ark of gopher wood. Because the instructions were very specific, and the

Sixteenth-century illustration of the unicorn at sea.

The unicorn is too proud to board the ark in this woodcut by Tobias Stimmer dated 1576.

ark very large, it took Noah and his three sons some time to complete the vessel and make it seaworthy. When at last it was done, Noah gathered all the animals around him and chose a male and female of each kind. Of the birds he took seven of each so that later they could spread seed across the face of the earth. Noah's sons led the animals into the ark. They all went docilely, glad to have been chosen from all of their species, glad to be saved. From the smallest to the largest, from the flea to the elephant, from the yellow canary to the grizzly bear, all the animals filed up the wooden gangplank and into the hold.

When the rains began to pound, in a steady, heavy cataract of blame, the ark rose with the water, and the ship began to rock. Inside the ark, the animals were locked in cacophonous darkness. But the unicorn was not among them. And no one knows why.

Some say that, although all the other animals boarded the ark peaceably, the unicorn was rambunctious, prodding other animals with its horn, demanding more space, arrogantly lording itself over the other animals. Noah had been working hard. It was not easy fitting all the animals in, and his temper was short. When the unicorn began to prance across the turtle's back and taunt the lowly worm, Noah became irritated and, in a fit of pique, demanded that the unicorn leave the ark. A few minutes later he regretted his decision. He climbed down from the ark and searched the nearby groves, calling repeatedly to the one-horned beast. But the unicorn had galloped off into the dark clouds on the horizon, and it did not return.

Others say the unicorn was too big to fit on the ark. The unicorn was as large as Mount Tabor, the ancient rabbis said, and its head was almost ten miles long—only the tip of its nose would have fit on the ark. So when the water began to simmer, when steam rose from the ocean and met the rain as it ricocheted off the roily surface, the unicorn disappeared in the flood.

Then there are those who claim the unicorn was so arrogant that it refused to enter the ark at all. Instead, for forty days and forty nights the unicorn swam in rising seas, its back pummeled by coal-colored rain. Sometimes it swam close to the ark as that pitch-covered, creaking ship was tossed this way and that by the waves and the wind; other times the unicorn swam far off, its sides brushed by the curious frightened fish. But the unicorn was not afraid, for its strength was great. At last the rains stopped; the unicorn still swam. The sun broke through the dissolving clouds, and the waters became calm. Still the unicorn swam, for there was yet no land. When the waters began to recede, and Noah tossed the dove overboard to search for the olive branch, the unicorn was swimming still. For a week more, the unicorn swam; and finally, the dove returned to the ark with a leaf in its mouth. Then Noah opened the warped and salty doors, and the birds flew up in a multi-colored cloud. They flew in all directions, searching for land, but there was no land in sight yet—only that single olive tree three days' journey away. And so a few birds perched upon the unicorn's horn and were followed by others. The long-tailed falcon lit upon the horn; then the ruby-throated hummingbird, the golden eagle, the egret, the tangerine finch and the opalescent pigeon, the squawking jay and the gull, the auk and the tern and the cuckoo, the mockingbird, the blackbird, and the grackle, and a host of sparrows. And as the birds rested their airy bodies upon the horn, the unicorn began to sink. It had trouble keeping its head up, and it shook its horn desperately from side to side. But the birds, restrained for so long in the rolling ark, were used to such movement and thought nothing of it. And the swallows came with their small square heads, and the warblers, and the flame-colored oriole; the kite, the owl, and the woodpecker joined them and so did the duck, the goose, and the whistling swan. The unicorn sank further, the murky waters lapping about its oval nostrils, and then about its wide and terror-stricken eyes, which also disappeared beneath the waves. For a moment, the horn alone broke the surface of the water, but then it too sank, and all at once the birds flapped away with a vast and windy turn of wing, rippling the water about them. They had spotted land.

Fourteenth-century miniature in Queen Mary's Psalter. The animals and birds gather around the ark along with members of Noah's family.

II
THE EASTERN BEGINNINGS

Before the creation the universe was like an egg, with heaven and earth mixed up inside. When the shell finally cracked open, chaos spilled in all directions. It took P'an Ku, the first man, eighteen thousand years to create the universe out of the confusion. Each day, with mallet and chisel, he chipped away at the light and the dark and the five elements, and each day he grew six feet. In his work he was assisted by the four most fortunate animals: the dragon, the tortoise, the phoenix and the unicorn. When his task was completed, P'an Ku died. His body became the world: his blood was water, his flesh was earth; his breath turned to wind and his voice to thunder; his eyes became the sun and the moon. His bones were stone and his marrow gold, his hair was vegetation; his beard became the constellations, and his sweat turned to rain. Each animal then sought a territory of its own. The dragon swam into the seas. The tortoise (which is always female and can mate only with a snake) crawled into the swamp. The phoenix flew to dry land. And the unicorn, which in China is

Detail of Ming Dynasty painting, Lohan Moving Through Fire and Sea, *ink on paper, sixteenth or seventeenth century.*

known as the k'i-lin, galloped into the green forests.

These four auspicious animals inhabit hidden realms, where their strength is undiminished by contact with human beings. Only occasionally do they show themselves. The unicorn's special times are two. When the ruler is just and kind, and the times peaceful and prosperous, the k'i-lin appears in a glade as a sign of good fortune. But when a great leader is about to die, the k'i-lin appears as an omen of loss.

Five thousand years ago, Fu Hsi, the emperor, was sitting by the bank of the Yellow River. The river, which had been pocked with rain, seemed calm and sluggish. The gray-green willow, whose branches had lashed in the wind like the whips of charioteers, now bent almost to the river's edge. The day before, water churned against the shore and the air was split with lightning. Now, even the dragonflies were still. The tumult of the previous day was nowhere to be seen. And so it is with humankind, the emperor mused; the thoughts and ideas which shape our lives die with us, and nothing remains. He reached forward to pick up a pebble by the river's edge, and as he did so the water splashed upon his wrist. Raising his eyes to see what had created the disturbance, he saw the k'i-lin. It resembled a calf but was covered with gleaming scales like a dragon and from its forehead grew a silvery horn. It was wading carefully through the rocks in the river, and although the water was muddy, everywhere the k'i-lin stepped the water became clear, slightly green like heavy glass, with the stones on the river bottom sparkling like emeralds. When it stood directly in front of Fu Hsi, the k'i-lin stomped its hoof three times upon a rock.

The words on this painting tell a slightly different story about Confucius's mother. "Before Confucius was born his mother . . . was walking with two maids in front of her house. Suddenly a k'i-lin appeared . . . and she hung a fine thread over its horns, whereupon the k'i-lin appeared entirely contented. It then walked around her three times and disappeared. Soon after that she became pregnant and eleven months later bore Confucius. Since ancient times the k'i-lin is said to have appeared before the births of all great men in China . . . as if to herald the coming of a great personage." Traditionally the animal has only one horn, but sometimes it is presented differently.

月懷信綵興素纖曰闕吐時先送麒
而姓宿繫之王裏水里有玉有聖子麟
生十而角繡顏遷精其麒書麒未圖之
  一去 氏衰子文麟於麟生麟麟
       周而
       而

Its back was covered with magic signs and symbols. The k'i-lin spoke to him but once, in a voice like a monastery bell, and began to walk away toward a distant grove. Fu Hsi stared at the lines and squiggles on the beast's back until the distance made them indistinct. Then he grabbed a stick and traced the symbols in the dirt. From these symbols would come the first written language of his people, and although all his generation and all generations afterward must die, their thoughts and ideas can live forever through the gift given to Fu Hsi and China by the unicorn.

Fu Hsi's reign was an illustrious one, so it was fitting that the k'i-lin should appear to him. The emperor introduced hunting, fishing and the care of flocks to his people, and he invented the first musical instruments and the trigrams, which later were used in the *I Ching* for divination. The next emperor, Shên Nung, who discovered the medic-

inal properties of plants, never saw the k'i-lin, but his successor, Huang Ti, did. Known as the Yellow Emperor, Huang Ti regulated the calendar and was the first builder of houses and cities. A practical man, he increased the size of the empire and he expanded commerce—partially out of a strong economic sense, partially out of his love for luxury. As he grew older, the pleasures and comforts that await a revered old man became more important to him. One day Huang Ti sat in his garden wrapped in an embroidered robe and, as sometimes happened, his mind wandered back to his young days and to his favorite consort, who had invented the manufacture of silk. He remembered her smooth brow and soft tread and the way she would hover over the mulberry bush to pick its fruit. The garden now was fragrant with chrysanthemums. Several workmen were digging with short spades at the roots of a boxwood tree. Sud-

The k'i-lin, after a nineteenth-century Chinese painting.

denly one of them shouted out. Huang Ti turned around and saw in front of him, by the mulberry bush, the k'i-lin, with a horn the color of pearl. "Yin-shing," it cried, and its voice rippled out like chimes. "Yin-shing, Yin-shing." The workmen knew the meaning: The sage will be accompanied on his journey, they thought. And so it was that shortly afterward, Huang Ti died and he rode into eternity on the back of the k'i-lin.

Two thousand years later, a young woman called Ching-tsae wandered through the hills of Lu searching for an ancient temple perched on a low, dry hill. Her feet felt warm and swollen, and when at last she reached the temple, it was smaller than she remembered and looked deserted. She made her offerings and settled in a cool, dark corner. Her eyes focused on a carved mandala and her breath grew slow and she fell into a trance. Five old men appeared before her then. They called themselves the colors, the elements, the planets. From behind an altar they led an animal with a single horn. Nuzzling her hand, the mysterious beast slipped a tiny piece of jade into her palm. It was the time of the Chou dynasty, and the k'i-lin had not been seen since the days of Huang Ti. Yet Ching-tsae remembered the scraps of old stories and knew it for an omen. The old men vanished; the k'i-lin stood before her and lowered its head to her lap. For several hours, in the corner of the temple, she stroked the gentle head of the k'i-lin, and the air shimmered like water and was filled with the scent of cinnamon. At last Ching-tsae pulled a white embroidered ribbon from her hair and tied it around the horn of the k'i-lin. As she did this, she suddenly felt woozy; for a second her eyes closed, and the k'i-lin vanished. Ching-tsae waited, but neither the unicorn nor the five old men reappeared. When she returned home, the sun had set long before and her small daughters were asleep. She quietly lay down next to her husband, Heih, told him what had happened, and showed him the piece of jade. On one side it was smooth and green, on the other an inscription had been carved. She whispered the words to Heih: "The son of the essence of water shall succeed to the withering Chou and be a throneless king."

Heih was an old man, and it was very late, but when he heard the inscription he rose to his feet and strode into the garden, where he began to

Two Chinese porcelain k'i-lin, taken from a mold of the K'ang Hsi period (1662–1773) and made during the late Ch'ing Dynasty (1644–1911).

Iron kirin.

pace. Beneath the heart-shaped leaves of the catalpa tree, he and Ching-tsae discussed the prophecy and what it might mean. It was clear to both of them that they had been singled out, but for what, they did not know.

Every day after that, Ching-tsae would hold the jade in her hand, hoping to summon the unicorn. She returned to the temple many times, where she threw the yarrow stalks to consult the oracle, and often she felt dreamy and distracted. Once she thought she saw something out of the corner of her eye, but when she whirled around to catch the wispy phantom nothing was there; it was only silk fluttering in a sudden breeze. Harvest came. There was wind, then cold, then dust. In the middle of winter, her baby was born. He was known as K'ung Fu-tze, or Confucius, and Ching-tsae told him the story of the k'i-lin many times.

When Confucius was an old man, a duke in the realm of Lu went on a hunting expedition and captured the k'i-lin. Word came immediately to Confucius, who even in his lifetime was recognized as a great teacher and philosopher, and he went to see the animal. It was fenced into a small area with rough wooden slats, which he leaned over in order to see the k'i-lin as closely as possible. It looked at him directly with sad, clear eyes. Around its horn he saw his mother's white embroidered ribbon, and he grew afraid. "For whom have you come? For whom have you come?" he cried. He knew the k'i-lin was not there to herald a golden age, for it was a time of weakness and confusion. It must be, then, that the k'i-lin had come to announce the death of a great man. Confucius had had a dream of death—he had seen the crows at dusk—and although he did not fear death, he did not welcome it either. Death was all around him. A son had died, and two beloved disciples as well, and the k'i-lin was standing captured in a yard with a ribbon around its horn. He knew that the k'i-lin had come for him. "The course of my doctrines is run," he said.

So Confucius took to his bed. "The great mountain must crumble. The strong beam must break. The wise man must wither away like a plant," he said. Yet the dying was not easy, and more than a week passed by while Confucius quietly waited in his bed, with neither rice nor prayer to sustain him. When he died, a hundred disciples built straw huts of mourning at his grave and remained there for three years. Afterwards, the Chou dynasty continued its decline and eventually perished. But the influence of Confucius is still felt. Many dynasties decorated his grave with imperial tablets honoring his wisdom, and even today school children know his name. He was as powerful as a king, although he never occupied a throne.

Many years passed before the unicorn was seen again in China. Four hundred years after Confucius, Wu Ti, an emperor of the Han dynasty, saw the k'i-lin on his palace grounds. It was just a

glimpse, seen among the trees at dawn. But because nature was in balance and times were good, Wu Ti, who was a just and beloved ruler, was sure the unicorn was there to attest to the perfection of his reign. He longed to see the animal again—perhaps even to capture it—and in order to attract it, he began the construction of a beautiful pagoda to honor the k'i-lin. Everyone assured Wu Ti that his reign was a blessed one, especially since he had managed to win so many military victories against the barbarians in the north. But Wu Ti never saw the unicorn again, and this became the chief disappointment in an otherwise happy life.

Dragon, lion, and k'i-lin. This sixteenth-century Eastern work illustrates the rivalry between the lion and the unicorn, a popular theme in the West.

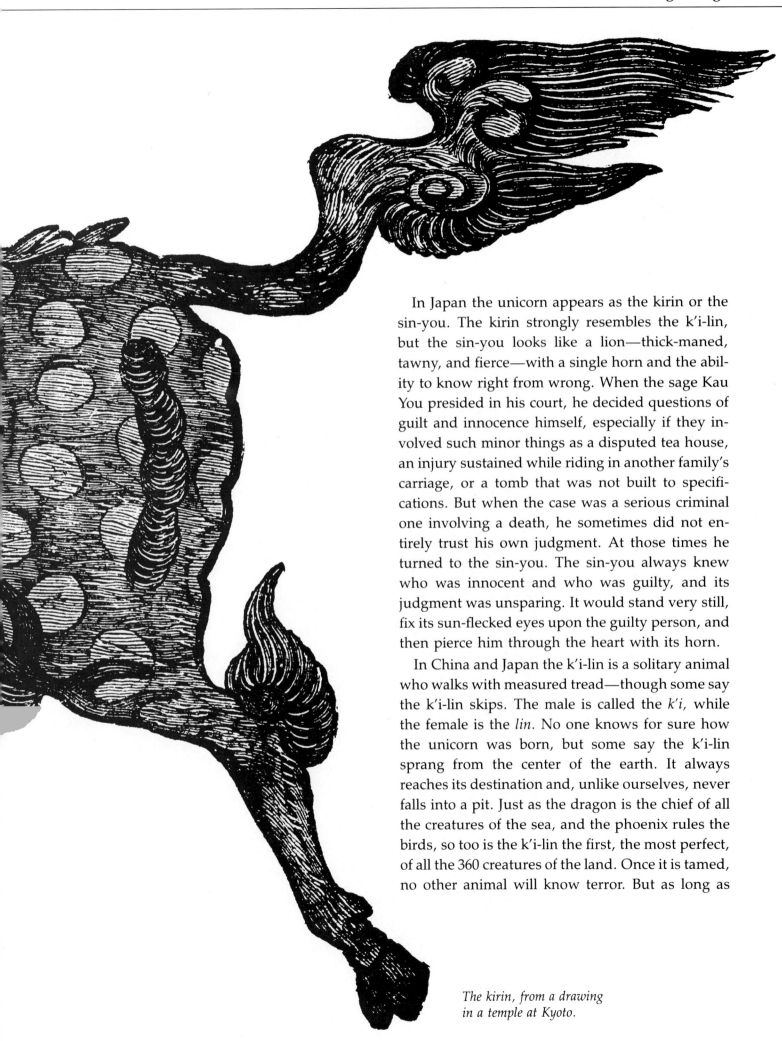

In Japan the unicorn appears as the kirin or the sin-you. The kirin strongly resembles the k'i-lin, but the sin-you looks like a lion—thick-maned, tawny, and fierce—with a single horn and the ability to know right from wrong. When the sage Kau You presided in his court, he decided questions of guilt and innocence himself, especially if they involved such minor things as a disputed tea house, an injury sustained while riding in another family's carriage, or a tomb that was not built to specifications. But when the case was a serious criminal one involving a death, he sometimes did not entirely trust his own judgment. At those times he turned to the sin-you. The sin-you always knew who was innocent and who was guilty, and its judgment was unsparing. It would stand very still, fix its sun-flecked eyes upon the guilty person, and then pierce him through the heart with its horn.

In China and Japan the k'i-lin is a solitary animal who walks with measured tread—though some say the k'i-lin skips. The male is called the *k'i,* while the female is the *lin.* No one knows for sure how the unicorn was born, but some say the k'i-lin sprang from the center of the earth. It always reaches its destination and, unlike ourselves, never falls into a pit. Just as the dragon is the chief of all the creatures of the sea, and the phoenix rules the birds, so too is the k'i-lin the first, the most perfect, of all the 360 creatures of the land. Once it is tamed, no other animal will know terror. But as long as

The kirin, from a drawing in a temple at Kyoto.

humanity is besmirched by greed and anger, as long as there is war and hunger and disease, the unicorn will remain hidden and wild. In evil times, the k'i-lin does not appear.

And so the k'i-lin was not seen in the Middle Kingdom. Centuries of disunion came and went; the Sui and T'ang and the Sun dynasties were established, flourished, and died. Mongol invaders conquered China and for almost three centuries the Ming ruled. Among them was the Emperor Yung Loh. His father, the first ruler of the dynasty, had unified the realm. Yet when Yung Loh came to the throne, the plague of violence returned like a swarm of locusts, and many men and women perished. Yung Loh was a builder who filled the cities with palaces and temples. He also sent many ships to Ceylon, to Java, and to Africa, where the merchant vessels loaded up with goods unavailable and unimagined in China. When the sailors reached the coast of East Africa in 1415, it was the longest journey they had ever undertaken. They disembarked at the first possible moment and began to meet the people. Because this country was very different from China, not least of all in its flora and fauna, the Chinese sailors were more than a little surprised to hear the people talking of an animal with a name very like that of the k'i-lin. Even the description sounded similar; the creature had the body of a deer, a long neck, and a single horn in the middle of its forehead. It was a graceful, gentle beast that seldom spoke and was given to hiding in groves of mimosa. Perhaps this was the ancient

Iron kirin.

OPPOSITE
Iron kirin, used as an incense holder.

k'i-lin. Alas, when the sailors saw it, some small doubt crept into their minds, for the African animal stood eighteen feet tall. And although the unicorn is normally so sensitive it will neither tread upon an insect nor eat fruit before it falls, this animal was distinctly observed, by more than one sailor, crushing shiny beetles as it galloped along the river and eating the red berries of the gob tree. Still, the sailors were excited and decided, despite the difficulties, to take the animal back to Yung Loh.

Months later they landed in China and presented the animal to the emperor. Yung Loh knew right away it was not a true unicorn, but he accepted its appearance as a great honor anyway, and to demonstrate his appreciation, pronounced it a k'i-lin. It did not matter, really; the giraffe was every bit as strange and wonderful as a k'i-lin would have been, and Yung Loh was a good ruler, deserving of praise. Perhaps the real k'i-lin was offended by this substitution, or perhaps a truly superior leader has not been born since Wu Ti. In any case, the k'i-lin never returned.

Although the k'i-lin never reappeared, in Annam, then a part of southern China and now Vietnam, the people held a yearly unicorn dance. On the full moon of the eighth month, when the whole of creation was holding its breath waiting for the monsoon to start, they would put on costumes and masks. When spirits were high and identities hidden, the archers tied an effigy of the unicorn to a platform and shot at it. And they sang this song:

The unicorn's hoofs!
The duke's sons throng.
Alas for the unicorn!

The unicorn's brow!
The duke's kinsmen throng.
Alas for the unicorn!

The unicorn's horn!
The duke's clansmen throng.
Alas for the unicorn!

They aimed first at the
hoofs, then at the brow,
and then at the horn.
Their breaths were warm
behind their heavy masks,
and their cries raucous—
and shortly afterwards,
the rains would begin.

صورتكركدان

ابو اکرسِ كركبن

کرکدن را زهمه جانوران ازین جنس بعددکمترست و جزنکی نزاید و آنجا کی زنده ماند و تومذکازاستی او

III

THE FIERCE KARKADANN

For six thousand years, Gayomars, who was made of light, lived in harmony with the bull and with the earth. Gayomars was the sun, whose fire was undiminished; the bull was the moon, whose light was always changing; and the earth loved them both. The earth and the bull were lovers, and from their union came the kine. Then the earth embraced Gayomars and gave birth to the rhubarb bush, thick-stalked and reddish. From the roots of the rhubarb sprang Siyamak and from the flower, his son Hushang. Cattle roamed everywhere, melons grew in the valleys, and the date palm provided shade and sustenance. Throughout the kingdom there was peace, until the scales of Libra tipped out of balance and shadows fell across the land.

Then the demon divs emerged from the center of the earth to wage war. They poisoned Gayomars and the bull with the night-colored iris and threw them to opposite sides of the sky. A div with an iron mace crushed Siyamak's skull. Thus Hushang, who saw him die, became king on the battlefield.

The karkadann, from a thirteenth-century Manāfi'-i hayavan *manuscript.*

Filled with grief and anger, he avenged the murder of his father by shooting the div who had killed him with an eagle-feathered arrow. Then he showered balls of hot metal upon the divs and drove them away. But still he mourned. One day, beneath a hot, flat sky, he threw rocks at the face of a cliff. A sharp-edged obsidian crystal hit a boulder and, in a ring of sparks, cleaved it in two.

Inside the boulder was a savage and ungainly animal. Red eyes glinted on either side of its broad head, and its tail was thick and fleshy. Immediately it galloped away, across the dry plains of Jol, through stretches of land so desolate even the divs did not go there. When it reached the green river banks, the fetus growing inside of the beast poked its head out of the womb, grabbed a mouthful of sweet figs from a tree, and drew inside again. It grew rapidly until, at last, its strength was like a mountain's. Rending its mother's womb, it forced its way out for a final time. Her pain was great; it turned to rage when she saw that her offspring bore little resemblance to her. The whelp's body was like a rhinoceros's and its tail was like a lion's. Each leg had three yellow hoofs, one in front and two behind. From its forehead grew a black horn, curved like a crescent. In anger, the beast began to lash at her child with her rough and spiky tongue. The newborn, oozing blood from its mother's ministrations, galloped out of reach and escaped into the plains. In a new guise and demeanor appropriate to this fierce land, the unicorn had appeared again.

As in China, the unicorn was described differently by different people. But where the k'i-lin was a gentle creature, the karkadann—for such the unicorn is called in Arabia and Persia—is a war-like, violent animal, born in blood and vehement in battle.

For a century after the birth of the karkadann, it was dreaded by all living creatures and left thoroughly alone. When it grazed, other animals were careful to leave a distance of at least one hundred parsangs between themselves and the karkadann. When it bellowed in its corrosive voice, the birds flew away. But the elephant had never seen the karkadann and was not afraid.

During the last year of the reign of Hushang, some workers on the island of Roha were collecting the sap of the camphor tree. Camphor trees on Roha grew very high, and the men were in the top branches,

TOP
Unicorn on ancient glass vessel.

BOTTOM
The unicorn in a fifteenth-century Persian manuscript.

making the first incisions to bleed the tree dry. As they pulled their saws across the bark, they inhaled the warmth of menthol and listened to the screeching metal. Some of the workers heard the sound of hoofs approaching. They looked below, through the radiating branches of the evergreen, and saw the karkadann. They were high up, the air was heavy with the soporific camphor, and the karkadann did not see them. It leaned against the tree with its thick, jointless legs, and rested quietly.

An elephant, separated from its herd, grazed nearby and, likewise lulled by the camphor, stumbled into the camp. For the first time, the karkadann and the elephant saw each other. Instantly they tasted hate and fear. The elephant roared through its sinuous trunk; the men in the tree could see the cloverleaf tip of the trunk as the elephant held it high. The karkadann stomped upon the ground with its front legs and the elephant flapped its enormous, sail-like ears. The karkadann sharpened its horn against a rock until it glistened like a scimitar, and the elephant charged. Its ivory tusks grazed the karkadann's neck. The karkadann turned and drove at the elephant's heavy flanks, but the trunk slapped the karkadann's head, and its horn stabbed the earth. The men in the trees clung to the branches vibrating from the blows of the beasts below. The elephant reared upon its giant legs. Then the karkadann raised its head, aimed its horn at the elephant's belly, and with a single thrust, impaled the pachyderm upon its horn.

The elephant's sounds were fearful, high and cacophonous, for it was dying. Yet the victory, the men saw at once, was a partial one. As much as the karkadann shook its head, it could not dislodge the elephant. The elephant's blood dripped down the sharp sides of the horn; in the heat of the sun, the elephant's fat, of which there was a good deal, melted and ran like butter into the eyes of the karkadann, where it congealed. Weakened and blind, the karkadann, with its huge burden, sank down into a pile of ropes and rugs left by the men near the tree. Then the enormous roc, whose egg alone is the size of the dome of a large mosque, flew overhead, flapping loudly and fanning the simoom winds. It swooped suddenly downward and, with its gigantic beak, picked up the karkadann and the elephant and flew away, above the valley of serpents and into the mountains, where it dropped

Persian miniature, about 1550, from the Aza'bibal-Mukhlugat. *The traditional enmity between the karkadann and the elephant ends with the elephant impaled upon the unicorn's horn.*

them into a cavernous nest. There the baby rocs made a brief but succulent feast of elephant and karkadann.

Men too have felt the point of the karkadann's horn—but men are craftier than the elephant and sometimes, in a battle against the unicorn, they win. One morning a young Bedouin left his home in the desert of northern Arabia to hunt the karkadann. He left with a camel, a bow and arrow, and a small sack of provisions. Only his twin brother knew his destination, and in exchange for secrecy, the young hunter had promised to his brother the face skin of the karkadann, to be fashioned into a quiver for his arrows. The hunter's intentions were not unworthy. He wanted to use the fat of the animal to cure his grandfather's arthritis, and with the flesh he hoped to exorcize the demons that had haunted his sister's sleep ever since she had gone to live in the tent of her husband.

When his twin had been gone for three, then four, days the brother at home, who had kept silent, began to worry. Finally he too took a camel and set out across the sand dunes to find the karkadann. After traveling many hours he came to an outcropping of granite, and there he saw his brother's leather sack in a puddle of dry brown blood. Falling to his knees, he prayed for help in finding his twin. When he arose he saw, on the horizon, the karkadann—this time shaped like a graceful, one-horned oryx—with a man draped across its back and impaled through the thigh with the long, curved horn. The animal was tossing its head and trying to dislodge the hunter, who moaned with every movement. The Bedouin called out his injured brother's name; the karkadann lifted its head and began to charge, but because of the weight on its horn, it could not reach the man and his camel.

That night the young man returned and searched again for the karkadann and his brother. When he sighted them he stood still and waited until his brother, in his agony, turned his head and saw him silhouetted against the stars. He aimed his bow and arrow but could not shoot for fear of hitting his brother. Instead, he held a silver dagger high in the air until it glinted in the moonlight, and he placed it carefully in a patch of grass where, per-

haps, the karkadann would graze. And he waited.

In the morning, the karkadann, with the brother still impaled and clinging to its back, wandered near the tall grass and as it did so, the Bedouin reached down, grabbed the knife, and stabbed the karkadann between the ribs. Screeching, the karkadann stumbled, then righted itself. Its front legs buckled and it fell forward, shaking its head. Its back legs gave way. The beast exhaled a sour cloud and its hoofs twitched. Then it was still. The healthy twin joyfully helped his wounded brother off the horn and tied a piece of rough-woven cloth around his bleeding leg. They cut off the horn and took it, with the rest of the karkadann, back to the settlement, where the animal was put to excellent use. The fat was burned and rubbed on their grandfather's knuckles and hips, and the old man felt relief and was able to walk to the well. Meat on the karkadann's sides was used to exorcize their sister's demons; her sleep became clearer, and she danced at the feast where the karkadann was roasted for the tribal elders. No part of the animal was wasted, and no part was valued more than the horn, which was made into a flute known to charm both sheep and snakes and kept as well as a talisman against the bite of the scorpion.

The Bedouin brothers were not the only ones to kill the karkadann. Gustasp killed the karkadann in battle, and so did Bahram Gur, a follower of Zarathustra, who led his people to war against the Roman Empire. Isfandiyar killed two wolf-like karkadann in a single battle—but even these feats of strength and courage were nothing compared to those of Iskandar.

In his short life Iskandar conquered many people and carved an empire in the East. Yet stories about him include more than military exploits and political intrigues, for Iskandar, like King Arthur and Charlemagne, occupies a spot somewhere between history and legend. In the West, he is known as Alexander the Great.

Another Persian unicorn, from a thirteenth century miniature.

Iskandar first met the unicorn when he was a boy. Some noblemen had captured a unicorn and taken it to his father, Philip, as a gift. Philip, who was known for his ability as a horseman, had recently been injured and could not ride. He had tamed the greatest stallions in the country, and many of them were in his stables, but when he saw the unicorn—with the body of a horse, the head of a lion, and a single horn in the middle of its forehead—he longed to ride the beast and cursed his broken leg that disallowed it. Instead he turned to his many courtiers, the noblemen and warriors that populated his court, and offered the animal

Alexander the Great, on his unicorn, confronts the two-horned, bearded women.

itself and its weight in gold as a prize to him who could ride the karkadann. Many noblemen tried, but each in turn was thrown off by the wild and skittish beast. Iskandar sat watching by his mother's side. He saw how the would-be riders frightened the karkadann and how the noise of the crowd made it tremble. Then he left his mother, walked behind the barricades to his father's throne and asked permission to ride the animal.

Iskandar was only thirteen and small for his age. But he was cocky, and Philip was determined to teach him a lesson. So he allowed him to approach the karkadann. Unlike the others, Iskandar did not try to leap upon the animal's back and hold on to its neck. Instead he spoke to it softly, and stroked its lion's mane, and leaned against its side so it could feel the weight of his body. Eventually the creature's panic dissolved. Then Iskandar mounted the animal and cantered off.

Philip's pride at his son's accomplishment was tinged with a sense of foreboding. He feared Iskandar would become greater than himself. Nevertheless, he decreed that there be a celebration. That night there was revelry throughout Macedonia, and many men were killed in the jousts and duels and general carousing. From then on Iskandar rode the animal he named Bucephalus. He rode him into Thebes and Asia Minor and Persia. When Iskandar

was not with him, Bucephalus was kept in a cage for fear some ignorant foot soldier would try to ride him and lose his life in the attempt. With others, Bucephalus grew even more fierce; with Iskandar, he was gentle.

Iskandar rode Bucephalus into the land of the Amazons; he was on his famous mount when he fought the dog-headed men, and the giant women with horns, and the Cyclopes. And when he fought the wild hairy men, and the headless men, and the fire-breathing birds, Bucephalus was there, and also when Iskandar fought the wild elephants and the men of Arbela. But the toughest battle of all was waged against the deceiving divs.

After a series of long, bloody battles, Iskandar

Riding a unicorn, Alexander the Great happens upon the men with their heads in their chests.

and his men, now well into Persia, were delighted to find a lake where pelicans swept through the air and flamingoes stood sentry at the shore. The wind and the water and the orange-striped flowers of the tamarind tree were so relaxing to the men that they removed their armor and lay down on the shore. Almost at once they fell into a sound sleep. When they awoke it was dusk, and they were surrounded by beautiful naked sea nymphs with long pale hair and yellow eyes. Iskandar was approached by several of the most lovely, and he was about to embrace one of them when he decided, from long military habit, to see first how his men were doing. When he turned to look, the sea nymphs tried to hold him back. Iskandar pushed them aside and saw that they were not sea nymphs at all—not women at all—but were the divs, those same demons that had killed Gayomars and the bull and Siyamak, and had ever since been multiplying upon the earth.

The divs flew at him. He saw that those of his men who had embraced the sea nymphs had already died, their necks broken and their heads lolling. Iskandar shouted to his men, and Bucephalus reared up, trumpeting a harsh and horrifying sound, so that none of the men would be filled with desire and all would be filled with fear. Bucephalus charged into their midst and waved his horn. The sea nymphs dissolved into a yellow fog.

When the lake was calm again and the sun had set, Iskandar mounted Bucephalus for a tour around the camp and found that they had once again been surrounded by the demons—this time in the guise of a herd of horrible one-horned beasts. These animals resembled neither the rhinoceros nor the deer nor the horse. They had long, narrow skulls, like dragons, with shark-like teeth and tusks like the wild boar. Their tongues were serpentine, and from each forehead between the eyes rose a serrated horn. With their hissing bites and tearing

An eighteenth-century version of the karkadann. The horn on the nose illustrates the rhinoceros ancestry of the karkadann.

horns they were as quick to attack as the wild bees. Iskandar saw that these too were the divs, and although he was afraid, Bucephalus was fearless. With Iskandar upon his back, he rode into the midst of them. The beasts tore at his legs, but Bucephalus stood firm. When he lowered his head, with its single horn, they scurried away like lizards, for the demon divs cannot equal the strength of the unicorn. Again Bucephalus had saved Iskandar's life.

With all his victories Iskandar began to feel that he was unstoppable, and he announced to his generals that he would fly. They scoffed (although not to his face), but they did as he commanded and brought a throne and plenty of rope to a cliff above a tranquil lake. At the appointed time Iskandar rode Bucephalus to the chosen spot. Waiting there were a retinue of his men and a pair of griffins, half lion and half eagle, with tremendous white wings. The griffins were wild, and screaming loudly, but when they saw Bucephalus they calmed down and docilely allowed themselves to be strapped to the throne. Then Iskandar whispered a few words to Bucephalus and sat down on the throne, a griffin on either side of him. He took a golden spear from one of his men. On the tip of the spear was a large piece of raw beef. When he waved it in the air the griffins sniffed and grew attentive. Then he held it as high above him as he could. With the griffins beating their giant wings and straining toward the meat, the contraption rose in the air. Iskandar was flying.

Beneath him he saw the red roofs of the town—and then he could see the town no longer, but only swirls of white and green, and finally the earth itself looked like a hat floating on the ocean. The griffins had almost reached the stars when suddenly Iskandar was jolted by the sound of a heavenly voice that thundered at him. "Go back," it said. And he saw an angel and did not want to

A seventeenth-century adaptation of a Persian manuscript dated 1460. The karkadann waits patiently for the ring dove to alight on its horn.

return, but the spear with the meat on it was jerked from his hands and flung earthward. The griffins followed it at once. Iskandar held tightly to the arms of the throne as the earth swam back into view, and the griffins landed.

Iskandar looked around; the landscape was a strange one to him: it was thoroughly white. A white sun shone coldly upon a white expanse that curved to the edge of a forest where lances made of ice dripped from the branches of frozen trees. He thought he was going to die there, when Bucephalus bounded toward him. He mounted the unicorn joyously. Although they were many months' journey from home, and Iskandar's clothes had been torn to rags by the flight, they were back with his forces within minutes, for Bucephalus was faster than sound. No one ever saw the griffins again; and there are those that say the griffins were unnecessary, that Iskandar could fly by himself and often hovered above his camp on the night before a battle, while Bucephalus waited patiently below with eyes of light.

The karkadann is not always fierce and bellicose, like a rhinoceros or a rhino-wolf. At other times the karkadann is magical, like Bucephalus, or it may resemble a stag, a horse, or an antelope. The elephant is an especial enemy, and generally so is man—but the same is not true for woman, of whom this creature is extraordinarily fond. It did not take the cruel and crafty hunters long to figure this out, and so began the practice of using a woman as a decoy to snare the unicorn.

The ploy worked best when a virgin could be found, but if this was for one reason or another not possible almost any young woman would suffice. She would be seated demurely in an apparently secluded spot. When the unicorn approached her, she would reach out a hand, and he would nuzzle it. Then she would unbind her breasts, and the unicorn would lick them and suck them, and if there was milk in her breasts, the unicorn would become quite drunk, and lower his horn to her lap, whereupon the hunters, hidden in caves and behind trees, would capture it at once, without resistance.

The plan did not always work; it was not easy for the hunters to find women willing to participate in their nefarious plans. And sometimes, after the unicorn had sported with the woman, she would grab its mane and throw her leg over its back and ride away, leaving the hunters far behind. The unicorn is capable of love.

In addition to woman, the karkadann loves the ring dove. When it hears her coo, it stands still beneath the nest and waits for the dove to land on its horn. For fear of scaring her, the karkadann moves not a muscle, but stands for hours awaiting the slightest attention. The ferocious karkadann can be a mild and tender-hearted creature.

The karkadann appears in many forms. The most remarkable is as monumental and magnificent as Mount Alvand. The creature has three legs, six eyes, nine mouths, and a golden horn. For sustenance it drinks the dew from green plants. Each mouth is the size of a cottage, its feet are as large as a thousand flocks of sheep, and the horn is carved with the outlines of humans and peacocks and cattle. When this karkadann puts its head into the water, all the female creatures therein become impregnated and all the evil creatures die and are thrown upon the shore. The waters become pure and fruitful. All opposites unite, and that which was separate is joined together. Plump quail scurry through juniper forests, and the desert blooms by day and night, and all human beings meet their shadows face to face.

The unicorn and other creatures on a page from the Persian anthology Munis al-Ahrar, *dated 1341.*

IV
THE UNICORN-BOY OF INDIA

Many years ago, during the time of the rishis, a young boy named Vibhandaka lived in a village with his family. Every day he and his brothers went about their tasks; they milked the goats, collected dung for fuel, and in the proper season they sowed the seed, transplanted the shoots, drained the rice terraces, and reaped the harvest. The family prospered. But Vibhandaka was not satisfied. One feast day, a parade came through the town. For the first time, amidst the elephants, the torchbearers and the dancers, Vibhandaka saw a holy man. He felt as if he had been drained and filled again. More than anything else he wanted to follow the sage.

But his mother and father would not let him go. His mother cried, his father looked at him reproachfully, and his younger brother begged him to stay with the family. Vibhandaka felt badly that his family was in such pain, and so he decided to stay; but from then on, whenever he went about his tasks, the memory of the cool eyes and saffron-colored forehead of the holy man would flash

A seventeenth-century painting of the animal kingdom from Mugal India. Imaginary creatures such as the dragon mingle with real animals.

through his mind, and he longed to be with him.

One day, when his mother was in the field picking the purple brinjal chilies, he followed her and spoke of his desire. She listened sadly and told him if he felt the same way in a year, he could go. That night he heard his parents whispering to each other. "A year is a long time for a little boy," his father said. "In a year, he will have forgotten everything."

The year came and went. Still he remembered, and once again the festival visited the town, winding down the dusty road with the sounds of cymbals and chanting and bells. Once again the sage was there, riding in a painted palanquin and looking out serenely over the assembled crowd. This time, Vibhandaka knew that he must go; perhaps he would not have another chance. So he went to his parents and told them of his decision. They both wept, and held him close. His mother told him to put on his best clothes. She annointed his hair with ghee and she gave him gifts for the master: rice, lime, jaggery sugar, and a garland of mango leaves. Then the boy waved goodbye and ran down the road toward the distant parade. He never saw his family again.

His master lived far away in a tiny ashram half a day's journey from the dark waters of the Yamuna River. At first his master ignored him—would not even look at him. Then, after a while, he let Vibhandaka do a few menial tasks. Finally, after several seasons had passed, the master allowed him to study with him. But although the boy tried to be virtuous in every respect, the master often scolded him and told him that the seed of corruption, dormant when dry, blossoms when watered by the innocent rain. And Vibhandaka tried all the harder to rid himself of impurity.

For many years he lived with the master and was content. When he washed the steps of the ashram, he felt light glimmer behind his eyes; when he carried the bowl of rice water and coconut to his master's feet, he knew the calm of complete surrender; when he fell asleep at night, on the hard woven mat, he closed his eyes and heard his breathing slow down, and yet, all night, he could feel the weight of the shadows cast by the moon as they moved slowly across his blanket.

And so it went for many years. The ashram, deep in the forest, was not large, and after a while, no new devotees came to it. The master grew old, and

spoke less frequently, which did not matter to Vibhandaka at all. But a few of the other disciples wandered away, and in time he was alone with his master. Seldom did his master speak, but the glow around him grew so strong that finally, even on moonless nights, the edges of his silhouette shone. Vibhandaka was happy and went about his many tasks with vigor and contentment.

But one morning, when he went to the well to fill a pail with water, he felt immediately that something was wrong. He remembered the tears in his parents' eyes when, so many years ago, he had followed the parade. He had not thought of them in so long that it was with some surprise that he recalled their sad faces. His mother, he remembered, wore a blue sari with a golden thread woven through it. His father had had just a tinge of gray in his hair. Vibhandaka looked down at his own long, straggly beard; he was probably older now than his father was then. And so, he thought, his brothers and sisters had probably gone on to marry, and his parents perhaps were no longer living. He ran his fingers across the cold stone rim of the well, and he splashed his face with icy water. Such thoughts were useless. He emptied his mind until

Illustrations from Jonston Johannes's manuscript, Theatrum universale omnium animalium, *1755. Rumors of unicorns seen in India and other distant lands often filtered back to Europe, where zoological drawings such as these had the stamp of scientific accuracy.*

it was as clear as mountain air and as wide as the Ganges at floodtime. Then he went in to see his master.

He pushed aside the curtain that shielded his master's sleeping quarters. The old man sat in the middle of his mat in a lotus position. His face was soft and peaceful, but his eyes were empty. Before he even touched him, Vibhandaka knew that his master had died.

And so, after he had washed his master's body, and built a pyre, lit the flame, and collected the ashes, he closed up the ashram, for it was no longer a place of joy to him. He wandered into the forest until he found a dark cave. For several years he lived there but he found no peace. Before, his mind had been silent, still, and without thoughts. Now he found that his mind teemed with images and sounds. He remembered words his master had spoken to him; he recalled other disciples, many of whom, like himself, were young boys when they first came to the ashram and men when they left it. He remembered his mother churning butter, and his father building a clay dam in springtime. The voices of his brothers and sisters came back to him, and the taste of the chapatis his mother made, and the bite in the air when she ground the chili peppers.

He would have been very lonely except for one thing. The animals often came to his cave and seemed to want nothing more than a gentle word or a stroke upon the head. He thought it was probably not right for him to spend so much time with them; he ought, he suspected, to devote more time to contemplation and meditation. But alone he felt no peace; with the animals, he sensed some of the spirit of his master. The parrots and the mynah birds and the chakora birds, who live on moonbeams, often brought him berries in their beaks. The tiger and the leopard would lower their heads for him to pat, and the rabbits were still under his thin hand. Nevertheless he thought of his master and of his family left behind so long ago, and he was lonely.

The worst times were during the rains. Inside the cave it was damp and cold, and the animals seldom visited. Small muddy puddles at the cave's entrance merged into ochre pools, and as the rain drummed down upon the granite, he heard the voice of Vayu in the roaring of the wind. Then he

longed for something that he could not name.

One year, during the rains, he suddenly gave a tremendous sigh, and in that sigh he felt himself surrender. He needed nothing, he was sure. The cave was more than sufficient for his small needs. He had been fortunate. He felt his heart open up like a lotus, and he saw a shadow fall across the puddles. At the mouth of the cave was an animal like a gazelle, with thin graceful ankles and luminous brown eyes and a single curving horn in the middle of its forehead. She was the most beautiful animal he had ever seen, and her body was made of warmth. The unicorn sat upon Vibhandaka's feet, and they became warm; and she licked his face with her velvet tongue, and he was overcome with warmth.

The unicorn stayed with him in his cave after that, and after a time they were married. It was a Gandharva wedding. Kama, the god of love, and Rati, his wife, were the attendants. The six seasons were the guests, who brought green pomegranates and plantain leaves. And Vayu, the god of wind, sang in the trees, showering them with the lavender blossoms of the jacaranda.

Vibhandaka was happy, and soon the unicorn bore him a child. It was a boy with golden brown skin and deep brown eyes—human in every way except for a horn in the middle of his forehead. They called him Rishyashringa. He grew up knowing the language of animals as well as the language of humans. Vibhandaka thought that perhaps the soul of his master had entered the body of his child, for the boy was a perfect being, above reproach, without blame. They lived happily in the cave for many years.

One summer day, when Vibhandaka was a very old man, the unicorn began to shiver and burn. She lay upon a bed of leaves deep within the cave, and although Vibhandaka nursed her, rubbing balm into her flanks and feeding her tea made from mint leaves boiled in a clay pot, her eyes became cloudy and, at last, she died. He lay beside her still body and felt, not grief, but emptiness and longing. He touched her golden coat and the shadows that her lashes cast upon her cheeks; and his breath grew softer, slower, until it stopped altogether and he felt himself lift out of his body and float up to the ceiling of the cave, where, looking down, he saw the body of a white-haired, wizened old man clasping to his breast a golden unicorn.

Afterward, Rishyashringa lived alone in the forest. Occasionally, a visitor would wander through the woods and bring back stories of the unicorn-boy. It was said that all animals were tame around him, that fire and rain would do his bidding, and that when he plucked a leaf from a plant, two more grew in its place. But he had no interest in demonstrating his powers, nor in moving to the city. He was content in his father's cave, alone.

At that time, the king was an evil man who worshipped only gold and the spoils of war. Disdaining all the gods, he thought only of pleasure for himself. He had many slaves and fought in many battles, always without kindness to those who were defeated. Because he was so cruel he was punished by the gods; Britra, the dragon of drought, breathed upon the land. The sky burned blue and the rains no longer fell. Slowly the crops wilted and turned brown; the hills and the hollows grew dry, and sometimes they burned, black earth and smoke billowing to the horizon. Cows wandered the streets with their skin loose around their great curving ribs; their udders were empty. Children starved; their bellies were round and distended, their hair turned the color of dry straw, and their eyes were blank. For miles around the only sounds to be heard were the moaning of mothers, the whimpering of the dying, and the screeching and cawing of the buzzards and crows. The king's wise men, long banished to the dungeons for failing to make rain, urged him to call upon the unicorn-boy. But the king would not, for his pride was too great.

Thus it was that the king's daughter Shanta took it upon herself to search for the unicorn-boy. For luck, she touched the red kumkum powder to her forehead. Then she journeyed many miles by herself across the devastated country. Every time she saw a starving child, or a dying animal, or a field baked dry by the sun, her resolve was strengthened. Her long black hair was full of burrs; her feet were toughened with calluses and scars. But she followed the Yamuna River to its source and fought her way through the thick forest until she reached the cave.

No sooner had she opened her mouth to state her request than the unicorn-boy, who had never seen a woman before, fell in love with her. Yet he did not want to accompany her, for he had lived

Eighteenth-century bronze from Nepal, used as a temple guardian.

his entire life in the forest and did not want to leave it. Her solemn words disturbed him, though, and he felt confused.

One morning, after Shanta had rested for a day or two, she set out for the river, and, silently, Rishyashringa followed her. At the river she sat upon a raft, dangling her feet in the water—considerably less deep than it once had been—and, lifting her arms, loosened her long hair. She combed it until it was smooth and washed it in the water, and as she washed her hair, the unicorn-boy watched her through the dark leaves and fragrant yellow blossoms of the kadamba tree. He was very still, and never more so than when she unwrapped her sari and, still kneeling on the raft, began to cleanse it in the river. She spread it out to dry on the gray

boards of the raft, and she scrubbed her own body until it was glistening and lustrous in the sun. Then she lay beside her sari on the raft to dry herself. And all this time the unicorn-boy was watching. He was overcome by her beauty, by her long brown legs and round breasts, and he knew he should stay hidden behind the kadamba tree and be very still. After a while, Shanta pulled her sari around her and spread her hair upon her shoulders; and then, unable to restrain himself any longer, Rishyashringa approached the raft. Quiet as he was, she heard him moving through the undergrowth, and she stood up and turned to face him. In one hand she held a long staff, its end resting in the water. He stepped upon the raft, his face flushed. She lowered her eyes. Then he stretched his hand

out to touch her gentle chin, and as he did that, she pushed the raft away from the shore as hard as she could. It whirled in a sudden eddy and began to float downstream. Her hair blew about her face like black silk, and the unicorn-boy was so electrified that he did nothing to bring the raft ashore but allowed it to float until the river turned to dust.

All night they walked, through the forest and the fields, until at last it was dawn, and the seven purple horses that are the days began to pull the sun across the sky. Rishyashringa saw that the drought was as bad as she had said. Shanta led him to her father, the king, who scoffed at the single horn sprouting from the young man's forehead and did not believe that anything could be done. Pulling his daughter to his side, he called to his guards and demanded that the visitor be taken away. As the guardsmen approached, the unicorn-boy prayed aloud for rain. Before his prayer was done, the rain began to fall upon the parched land. The king fell to his knees and begged forgiveness of the gods.

For three days and nights it rained without cessation. When the hills began to turn green again, the unicorn-boy and the princess were married. Shanta wore silver ankle bracelets, and her palms were painted. Intricate designs made of rice powder covered every doorway, and from dawn to dawn the court musicians played their sliding ragas upon the sitar and the tabla and the flute. In their wedding tent the unicorn-boy and Shanta drank

A seventeenth-century Tibetan unicorn, kneeling to listen to the Buddha. The horn symbolizes the unity of Nirvana.

the green-tinted soma. Everywhere the land hummed with celebration and with spring.

But the king was not happy. He wandered disconsolately around his palace, afraid that he would be deposed, afraid that his daughter was plotting against him, afraid of growing old. One warm night he had a dream. A ferocious unicorn was galloping toward him, and no matter how hard he ran, he could not escape from it. At last it was almost upon him—he could see the pulse in its throat—and he jumped into an abyss, grabbing a flowering bush as he fell and landing on a narrow, crumbling ledge. Below, a dragon as shiny and hard as lacquer breathed flames upon him. Above, the unicorn bared its teeth and snarled at him; beneath its translucent skin he could see its skeleton. Four serpents emerged from crannies in the wall and slithered toward him. With bleeding fingers, he clung to the bush, but two mice, one black and one white, gnawed at its roots, and he could feel it pulling away from the rock. He turned his head slightly to see if there was, perhaps, another bush to hold, and as he did this, he saw upon the branch a few quivering drops of honey. He forgot about the danger at once; he could think of nothing but the honey and how much he wanted to taste its sweetness. But just as he was ready to reach for it, he recalled the deep abyss and the dragon below, and he awoke with a start.

In the morning, the king went to his astrologer, Barlaam, and told him the dream. Barlaam lit a stick of incense. For a long while he said nothing. Then Barlaam told him what the vision meant.

"The unicorn," he said, "is death, which follows us everywhere when it is our turn to meet him. The abyss is the material world into which we fall at birth and from which we cannot escape. The bush represents human life; the mice are day and night, which continually nibble away at the roots of time. The serpents are the four elements of human life. The dragon represents hell. And the honey is the sweetness of surrender which we must know before we can die peaceably."

"Will I die?" asked the king, afraid.

Barlaam gazed at his parchments. "Arrange your affairs," he said. "When the dream comes again, open your mouth and let the honey drip upon your tongue."

For two nights the king did not allow himself to sleep. Avoiding the eyes of the unicorn-boy, he placed his crown upon his daughter's head. Then he locked himself in a small temple where he spent the hours on his knees listening to a monk chant puja. The third night, however, he knew he could stay awake no longer. He bathed himself and put on his yellow silk robe. He did not want to sleep. But just for a moment, he thought, he would shut his eyes; and when he had shut them, he was once more being chased by the unicorn. He fell again into the abyss as Vayu howled around him. He clung to the rough branches of the bush. The mice were nibbling with their tiny rodent teeth; the bush was about to break. The snakes curled and turned in the dry earth, and the dragon's breath was sulfurous and foul. But when he saw the honey on the branch, the king opened his mouth to it. As soon as the sweet amber drop fell upon his tongue, the branch broke, and he plummeted into the jaws of the dragon, who tore his body apart. But he felt nothing, only the sweet stillness of the honey on his tongue, and the heavy, heavy weight of the yellow silk, cooling.

A copper engraving illustrating Barlaam's vision by Boetius A. Bolswerth (1580–1633). The unicorn represents death.

PART TWO

THE
MEDIEVAL UNICORN

V

THE HUNT OF THE UNICORN

From the eastern shores of India and the deserts of Arabia, the unicorn moved eastward into Europe, where its fame spread. Peddlers, who brought cumin and needles to the scattered, lonely villages, also carried with them tales of mermaids and kings and battles and the fabulous one-horned beast. In the walled cities and in the fiefs, in castles and monasteries and thatched huts, people who dug turnips or spun flax or cobbled shoes repeated these stories. No one was surprised when, occasionally, a hunter, chasing a stag through the forest, glimpsed something he thought was a unicorn through the branches of a distant tree. The sight of the snowy flanks, the quick grace, the silken beard and the mother-of-pearl horn would make him restless, dissatisfied with common prey. Back at home, the memory of the unicorn would linger, and he might speak of it to a few of his friends. After a while, the yearning grew so great, and the excitement so strong, that he and his friends would gather together with hounds and horns to hunt the unicorn.

The Unicorn in Captivity. *Chained to a pomegranate tree against a millefleurs background, the unicorn symbolizes the captured lover or bridegroom. Other interpretations view the unicorn as the risen Christ in Paradise.*

They met at dawn in the well-tended fields of the lord of the castle. The lord was there and several neighboring noblemen, as well as houndsmen, scouts, pages, and water carriers. A few even came who wanted to convince the hunters to leave the unicorn free and undisturbed. "Just as Adam and Eve were not permitted to touch the forbidden fruit," they said, "so are we enjoined against hunting the unicorn. Who knows what punishment awaits us if we transgress?" Their mission, however, was unsuccessful. While the haze of dawn still clung to the grass, the hunters organized themselves into several parties and went off in different directions to search for the unicorn.

The houndsmen ran ahead, their dogs coupled on leashes made of rope and leather. The greyhounds and the running hounds, who sniffed the air and the earth, raced silently over the loamy floor. An hour later a greyhound glimpsed, behind a hawthorn tree, the pale plumed tail of the unicorn and came to an immediate halt. A running hound then caught the cinnamon scent, and a page spied the silver hoofs sparkling in the violets. "Ho!" he called, and "Ho!" again, waving his arms toward the hunters. The unicorn had been sighted.

The hounds bounded through a thicket, following the unicorn's scent. Far behind them, weighted down with spears and swords, the huntsmen dashed forward in pursuit. A newly sprouted field, completely green, lay before them and they ran across the corner of it, trampling the tiny plants with their heavy shoes. But the unicorn was not concerned, for he knew the hunters could never hold him, and he even dallied a little out of playfulness and let them gain on him. The hounds swiftly crossed the vegetable garden and the orchard. Right at the edge of the wild wood they found the unicorn.

He was the color of cream, shaped like a small horse, with cloven hoofs and a long, spiraling horn. Behind him, a striped serpent edged along the banks of a stream. Clustered about the unicorn were other animals: the lion and the lioness, the hyena, the panther, the weasel, and the stag, all very careful not to touch the water, for the serpent had released its poisonous venom into the clear brook. Bending his knees the unicorn dipped the tip of his horn into the stream to purify it. For a moment the sun glinted across the water and the

Detail from The Start of the Hunt. *Three noblemen set out to search for the unicorn.*

stream gleamed like a mirror. Ducks and a wood-cock flapped into the water. The stag leaned for-ward to drink.

Watching this, even the fiercest of the hunters was momentarily calmed, for of all animals, the unicorn is the loveliest and most pure. In his shadow, the other animals were serene. And so the men watched in silence, without taking aim, peaceful in the uni-corn's presence, yet also aware that it would not be sporting to kill an animal without a chase. Then a huntsman raised the curved horn to his lips and blew a crescendo of high, braying notes. The unicorn

The Unicorn at the Fountain. *The participants in the hunt pause momentarily to watch the unicorn purify the stream by dipping his horn in the water so that the other animals may drink.*

perked up his ears and leaped across the stream. The peaceful moment had passed.

The other animals scattered, disappearing back into the woods. The unicorn ran on, ahead of the hunters, as swift as thought. He galloped across the meadow and then pranced into a grove of fruit trees, where the hunters lost sight of him. Beneath a cherry tree the unicorn paused for a moment. Then, trotting through the grove, he approached the stream, which had now widened into a river. Thinking the hounds would lose the scent, the unicorn waded into the icy water.

And the greyhounds did lose the scent. Even the running hounds with their noses to the ground lost the scent, though those with their noses in the air could still detect the warm and spicy odor of the unicorn, even above the cool river air. Baying and howling, the dogs plunged into the river and circled the unicorn. When the hunters rounded the border of the orchard they saw the unicorn gleaming in the river like the moon. One group of hunters came up along the east bank of the river; another crossed the footbridge and ran down the west bank. From all sides the hunters closed in, cutting off any escape route. The unicorn was surrounded.

The hunters aimed their spears at the unicorn's alabaster neck. He was theirs. And yet, some of them held back. To kill such a creature—even for the priceless treasure of the horn, worth more than gold—seemed wrong. The unicorn's coat was as soft and white as milkweed; the horn, of ivory and pearl, pointed toward heaven; the water lapping around his legs was clear, and the unicorn's silver hoofs glinted in the river. So some of the hunters were hesitant and their swords remained undrawn. Others pressed forward, their spears threatening. One hunter, partially hidden behind a thick bush, was so excited he could not wait a second longer and gave in to his desire to wound the unicorn. He pricked the snowy hide with the point of his spear and blood dripped into the water.

And yet—the unicorn had not been captured, could not be captured even though he was surrounded. He bobbed his head this way and that, looking for an escape. Then he reared out of the

The Unicorn Leaps the Stream. *Surrounded by hunters, the unicorn plunges into the stream.*

river; water fell from his body like diamonds. The hunters flinched under his fiery gaze, and when he lowered his head and began to charge at them, they darted to either side to avoid being slashed by the horn. A gap opened up in their midst, and the unicorn was free.

But the hounds were right behind, and once

The Unicorn Defends Himself.
*Outnumbered, the unicorn
gores a greyhound
and kicks a hunter with his
hind legs.*

again they circled the unicorn. The unicorn looked around wildly, surprised to see the hunters still so active in their pursuit. The wound on his back was smarting, and the hounds were nipping at his legs. The unicorn, who was a solitary animal, felt his breath quicken, and his heart leap, and his chest and neck suddenly flush. The men's eyes were harsh and glittering; the unicorn could smell their rotten breath and see the dark stubs of their teeth, and their voices sounded like the clanging of metal at midnight. From the center of his being, the unicorn felt in the pulsing of his heart something he had never known before. For the first time, the river of hatred flowed through his veins. He began to fight.

Suddenly surrounded, the unicorn kicked his powerful hind legs and gored a greyhound with his horn. The hunters surged forward with hoarse cries and poised spears, but the frightened dogs fell back and a dusty wind blinded the men. Again, the unicorn escaped. As a spear whizzed past him, he leaped away, bounding across the grassy field. Covered with sweat, filled with foreboding, the unicorn circled back toward the castle.

Just as the sounds of the howling of the hounds and the cursing of the men began to fade, the unicorn galloped around the castle and saw, in the fenced garden, three young women from the court. Two of them, sitting in the shade of an oak tree, were playing chess with a set carved of crystal. The third, slightly older than the other two and wearing a bright red dress, was picking red and white roses. Their beauty amazed him, and the sound of their voices was like bells. The unicorn noticed that the one in a red dress had a sly look on her face and, somehow, he did not like her. But the others were so beautiful he could not help but stop. As soon as they saw him, they exclaimed and put down their chess pieces; and yet, there was sadness in their voices, and he wondered why such creatures as these should feel so sad. One of them, whose auburn hair cascaded over a simple gown with russet sleeves, reached out a slim hand and combed the unicorn's curling mane with her fingers. He looked up at her, and saw that her brown eyes were filled with tears and that her pale companion at the chess table had averted her eyes. It was incomprehensible to him why they should act so strangely, and to comfort her he rubbed his neck against the maiden's arm. Out of the corner of his eye he saw the woman in the red dress suddenly raise her hand and wave it in the air. Perhaps he ought to run away, he thought; but the pleasure of the maiden's hand upon his mane was too great, and he tarried a moment longer.

Then the dogs were upon him, snarling and

The Unicorn is Tamed by the Maiden. *Legend says that the unicorn cannot be captured by force alone, but only by guile. In these fragments of a missing tapestry, the unicorn has escaped from the hunters. In an enclosed garden, a maiden caresses the unicorn, her fingers on his neck. But the dogs are upon him, and a hunter blows his horn to signal the others.*

FOLLOWING PAGE
The Unicorn is Killed and Brought to the Castle. *In the upper left, the hunters spear the unicorn. On the right, the lord and lady, along with a crowd of other people, are on hand for the arrival of the dead unicorn. Perhaps underscoring the religious symbolism, the lady wears a rosary and a cross, while the unicorn's neck is encircled by a thorny wreath of oak leaves.*

Madonna and Unicorn, *painted by the Spanish Forger. Here the parallel between the unicorn and Christ is made explicit. The houndsman with dogs represents the Angel Gabriel.*

puncturing his hide with their sharp claws and teeth. He leaped away from the maidens but the hunters cut him off. A cruel-eyed man lowered his spear—its point glittered in the sunlight, so close that the unicorn could see the splinters in the handle. The spear plunged forward and the unicorn felt lightning hit his side, and for a second the pain stopped, and he turned his head to look at the wound and at the women, who buried their faces in their hands. The pain surged into his side again and the blood flowed in a warm and heavy stream down his flank, and he rolled his eyes back in pain and sorrow. Just at that moment, the young man in front of him lifted his spear and plunged it into his neck. The dogs were gnawing at his back and pain filled his body like fire and he felt the fingers of the man behind him—a gentle fellow, who had not even brought a spear—close softly around the horn, to claim it.

The unicorn did not die easily. Blood poured from his body, and the red blood upon the white hide was brighter than the colors of the lord. But finally the unicorn was dead, his body not quite so luminous, the horn suddenly tinged with yellow. The hunters, who whooped and shouted and thumped each other on the back, lifted him up and draped him across a horse, who bowed his head and was more than usually still. Horns blew. The hunters shouted out for the maidens, but they were nowhere to be seen, so the men wound their way back to the castle. There the lord, in his red and white striped tights and crimson cloak, awaited with his queen the arrival of the unicorn. Among the members of the court gathered there was the maiden with the red dress. When the hunters called her name, she turned away from them and ran back into the garden.

Inside the castle everyone was excited. The servants, who were busy preparing a grand feast, peeked out the windows at the procession. Banners above the parapets fluttered in the wind; graceful swans drifted on the moat, and squirrels scampered in the hazelnut tree. The wreath of oak leaves which circled the unicorn's neck had already sprouted thorns. All in all, it was a festive day.

The three maidens still lingered in the garden. The one with auburn hair was especially distraught. Her friends tried to reassure her that the unicorn would have been killed anyway. The maiden in the red dress even gave her a white rose she had picked, yet she was inconsolable. From the castle the three women could hear the noise of the celebration, but they felt so despondent that instead of going inside they wandered along the path to the abbey.

From the castle, they could hear shouts and snatches of songs. Inside, in the great hall, the feast was still going on, and the three women could imagine that many of the celebrants were growing quite rowdy. The pale maiden shuddered at the harsh sounds that hung in the air. She could not bear to return there. When they reached the crumbling stone wall that marked the abbey lands, she recalled with sudden yearning her schooling there and the tranquil lives of the nuns. Opening the gate, she said goodbye to her friends and went inside.

The other two walked slowly back to the castle. "If only we had never entered the garden," mourned the maiden with the auburn hair. "If only we had refused to do this horrible thing. . ." The one with the red dress listened and nodded her head in agreement. But although she was very sad about the unicorn, she thought there was little purpose in dwelling on what could not be changed. And besides, she knew the floor of the great hall was strewn with fresh flowers for dancing. She bade her friend farewell and hurried back to the castle.

Then the maiden with the auburn hair, who had caressed the unicorn, was alone. Still holding her rose, she rambled through the grounds, castigating herself, until she came upon the stream where the unicorn had purified the waters. She splashed her face and hands with the cold water. For a long time, she sat there, until the sky in the west turned purple and the moon rose full in the east. In the fading light, she looked at the wilted rose in her lap. Already the edges of the petals were turning to parchment and the leaves drooped. She leaned forward and tossed it into the stream. As she did so, the moon glimmered against the waters and the nightingale sang its song and in the distance, beyond the orchard, she thought she saw the shining horn of the unicorn as it disappeared into the night.

VI
THE LION AND THE UNICORN

Throughout history, as far back as the Assyrians, the lion and the unicorn have been linked, for of all the animals the lion is the most majestic, and the unicorn is the purest. So it was natural that, when the king of Friesland wanted to give his daughter a wedding present, he gave her a unicorn. Even though she was a girl the king was proud of his daughter, for she was lovely, obedient, and adept at falconry. Consequently he did not anticipate the results his gift would have, for Isabel had always been a good and dutiful daughter, busy at her chores of weaving and embroidery. Her wedding was a festive occasion; troubadors played flutes and viols in a tent of blue silk, and bucketsful of silver coins were thrown to the serfs and lepers. Her husband was a powerful knight whose barony extended for many miles. In his youth he had gone on a crusade, and his piety even now was undisputed. Nonetheless, shortly after their marriage Isabel's behavior began to grow strange. She often galloped across the drawbridge on her unicorn, and all over the kingdom people

Smell, *from a series of tapestries called* The Lady with the Unicorn, *made about 1500. Five of the six tapestries in this set illustrate the senses.*

reported seeing the dark-haired princess racing through the meadows astride her shining mount. She liked to ride in autumn across the frosty fields to the river and sometimes in spring, with her falcon on her wrist, she rode the unicorn into the blossoming woods. She would have enjoyed spending even more time riding across the countryside, but one thing interfered: even though she was married and faithful to her husband she still possessed many suitors, in the courtly manner, and they occupied a great deal of her time.

Some of her suitors were wealthy, some were well-educated, some were loyal if nothing else, and some were handsome, but only one really interested her. His name was Bartholomew. He wore a black plume and carried her scarf with him wherever he went. In tournaments and jousts he invariably triumphed, and his adventures were many. The greatest of them all occurred one day in a distant forest, when a lion came up to the knight while he was asleep in a cave and began to maul him. Because he was wearing a hauberk of double mail Bartholomew was not injured, but the more he fought the lion, the more impressed by him he was. The lion was such a fierce and imperial animal that finally Bartholomew spoke to him, threatening to feed his horse on lion-marrow. At once the lion crouched on the ground beside him and, purring like a cat, nuzzled the side of his leg. Then the knight rode upon the lion, his horse trotting behind them. Forever after, Bartholomew was known as the Knight of the Lion.

Bartholomew continued to pay court to the Lady of the Unicorn. He wrote roundelays for her, brought her fruit and trifles, and tied her ribbon—interwoven with a lock of her hair—to his lance. One day, when the knight sought entrance to the castle in order to present his lady with a sheaf of poems, a page approached him at the drawbridge and told him that Isabel was dead. The knight cried out hoarsely. He threw his lance into the moat, and his helmet with the beautiful black plume, and the packet of poems, and he watched them sink into the brackish waters. He wept so hard and so long that his mouth was filled with salt, and he thought

Sight shows the lady holding a mirror to the unicorn, whose image is reflected in it.

BELOW AND OPPOSITE
Details from Taste. *The unicorn and the lion both support banners and wear capes bearing the coat of arms of the Le Viste family, who probably commissioned the tapestries.*

he would never recover. Unbelieving and distraught, he wandered beyond the castle walls for hours, and although a page and a watchman tried to talk to him their efforts were futile, for his misery was great. At last he mounted his lion and rode away toward the river in the woods where he had once met Isabel upon her unicorn.

In the meantime Isabel was inside the castle walls, and she would have been quite well but for an unfortunate visit she received from a messenger. Because the messenger wore black and gold livery she assumed he was in the service of the Knight of the Lion. His message was a most distressing one; he told her that the knight had been killed in a battle with marauding highwaymen. When she heard the news she moaned in distress and clasped her hands together. The messenger struck her on the head. She screamed aloud, but her cries could not be heard through the thick stone walls. She kicked at the messenger and pulled hard upon his beard, while he hit her again and again. Finally she passed out. The messenger picked her up, wrapped her in a patterned rug, and carried her from the castle. No one noticed his peculiar package, and no one barred his way. It was many hours before anyone became aware of Isabel's absence.

After tying her to the horse, the messenger rode away to his castle high on a cliff above a river. The castle was protected on three sides by the steep palisade upon which it was built, and on the fourth side it was guarded by a fire-breathing dragon. Inside the castle the atmosphere was dank and sorrowful. Inprisoned within, the Lady of the Unicorn mourned Bartholomew's death, and the sadder she felt, the angrier she became.

It was several days later when the Knight of the Lion, despairingly drinking mead at a tavern, first heard that Isabel had not died at all but had been abducted by someone masquerading in his own livery. Furious that he had been so fooled, Bartholomew mounted his lion and rode to the lady's castle to find out what had become of her. At the castle everyone was in mourning, and the lady's husband—who had ridden without success against the dragon and been seriously burned on one arm—had locked himself in a tower. So the knight turned away from the castle and followed the river to where Isabel was being kept hostage. The dragon, sleeping peacefully in front of the heavy iron doors of the castle, looked so formidable that the knight was afraid he would not be able to free his beloved. For a few minutes he rode back and forth through a cloud of mist on the road that led to the dragon and the doors, and he wondered what to do.

Then he saw, from a narrow inset window high on the castle keep, an arm waving a banner with the colors of the Lady of the Unicorn. Because he did not want to appear cowardly he immediately drew his sword and began to ride toward the dragon. The dragon blinked its bulging eyes and raised its head. Smoke streamed out of its high nostrils. It flapped its thick, fleshy tail on the road, and a cloud of dust rose up. When the knight put his spurs to the lion's sides, the lion sent out such a roar that the dragon arched its back, spread its scaly wings, and started to hiss. Dark, foul-smelling flames flared from its mouth, the air was filled with steam, and the knight veered away. The dragon breathed a long, hot wind in his direction, and although the lion's mane was singed the knight was safe. Turning his mount around he prepared once more to attack. He flashed his sword in the dragon's eyes, and the lion roared—but Bartholomew didn't get very close, for already he could feel the heat of the dragon's breath crisping his eyebrows, and his armor was unbearably hot. He tried to lunge at the dragon's midsection with his sword, and then again at the dragon's head, but the dragon was as quick as he was and the volcanic breath followed him everywhere. He was almost ready to give up and return later with a retinue of other knights when he saw below him on the road the translucent unicorn.

The unicorn was galloping as hard as it could, and its horn was glistening in the fog. The unicorn ran straight ahead, past the knight and the lion, and with lowered horn it speared the dragon in the middle, withdrew the horn, and prepared to attack again. The dragon reared up and exhaled flames upon the unicorn, but the flames sizzled off the unicorn's back as though it were made of ice. The dragon, infuriated, reached out a long-clawed paw to grab the unicorn. The unicorn dodged the saber-sharp claws and stabbed the dragon in the thickness of its haunch. Blood flowed thick and green. The dragon lifted its head to let out a mighty bellow; just at that moment the unicorn rushed for-

the island of Bute, bothered hardly at all with affairs of state and allowed others to rule for him. First his younger brother, the duke of Albany, governed. Then the king's elder son, David, ousted Albany from the regency. A bitter feud ensued. Albany regained his power and David died under mysterious circumstances. Some say he died of dysentery, some say of starvation; some say he died through "divine dispensation"—and some say he died with the willing assistance of his uncle, the duke of Albany. In any case Robert was alarmed. He sent his other son, James, to France to be educated, and he himself retired, once again, to Rothesay.

There he became totally despondent. Lame since 1388, when he had been thrown by a horse, he limped around the castle and stared out at the peaceful bay. The castle had been standing for over three hundred years, erected as a defense against the invader Magnus Barefoot of Norway. Through the centuries that followed Scotland fought with Norway and with England—not merely once, but repeatedly. In battle after battle Scotland tried to maintain her sovereignty through force, and through force the other nations tried to impose their own. And what came of it? Only death. Robert and his forebears ruled by violence and lived in fear. It was clear to Robert that Scotland could only achieve the peace and prosperity for which her people yearned through such purity and strength as that of the unicorn, the most virtuous of animals. And so he carved above a gateway two unicorns, one on either side of the royal arms of Scotland.

Robert did not live to see his dream realized. Shortly after the gateway was erected he learned that his son James had been captured at sea by the English. This bad news was more than he could stand, and he died almost upon hearing it. But the dream of harmony lived on, for the unicorns were incorporated into the royal seal of Scotland. Flanking the coat of arms, two unicorns, their necks encircled by the Scottish crown, ensured the survival of the dream, if not its realization.

Two centuries passed. In 1567, when Mary Queen of Scots was forced to abdicate, her infant son became James VI of Scotland. As a boy, James was weak, with a taste for learning that bordered on the pedantic. More than anything else, he abhorred violence—perhaps because there was so

✛ THE·ROYAL·ARMS ✛
As used officially in Scotland. Designed by A.G.Law Samson, ✛
Heraldic Writer to the Lyon Court, H.M.Register House, Edinburgh.

The Royal Coat of Arms as used in Scotland.

much of it in his childhood—and he was determined to avoid it if at all possible. He began to rule in his own right in 1583, and for twenty years after that he was a good and capable ruler.

In 1603, when Elizabeth I of England died, James was next in succession. As James I, king of both England and Scotland, he took the Scottish unicorn to England with him, where it shared the support of the British coat of arms with the traditional English lion. He had been an effective ruler in Scotland; he hoped that in England he would be able to achieve the peace that the unicorn represented.

But the English people took a dislike to him. They saw him as slovenly, coarse, undignified. More than anything else, they distrusted him because of his belief in the divine right of kings. "Kings are justly called gods," he said in 1609—a statement that did not endear him to his subjects.

James died in 1625. His reign had been marked by bitterness and strife.

It was not until 1707 that his two countries, Scotland and England, were officially united. Even then, the promise of the unicorn did not prevail, and many Scots continued to resent England. The presence of both the lion and the unicorn in the royal seal recalled an ancient legend, for just as Scotland and England had long been rivals, so too were the unicorn and the lion. At times, the two animals indulged their rivalry in a peaceful manner. Occasionally they played chess together, and when they did, the lion always checkmated the unicorn's king.

More commonly, they chased each other. The unicorn, whose nature is serene, never initiated these contests. It was the lion who, by dancing around the unicorn and snapping at her heels, fi-

nally irritated his rival so much that the unicorn, out of frustration, would be forced to chase the lion. The lion spurted ahead, over rocky hillsides and along river banks. The unicorn was always right behind, breathing her sweet breath on the lion's back; and unlike the lion, the unicorn did not tire.

But after a while, the lion became worried. The unicorn was angry, and her horn was menacing. So, like the rising sun, the lion leaped up and galloped across the sky until, at the very summit, he could look down upon the earth. But the unicorn was right behind, and the chase continued. When the lion had crossed the entire sky, as the sun was flattening on the horizon, he set foot again upon the earth, and the unicorn followed. The lion's legs were beginning to ache, and he saw that the unicorn was gaining rapidly on him. There was no chance for escape. The unicorn rushed toward him with lowered horn, and at the very last minute, the lion jumped behind a tree to hide.

The unicorn was startled, but she was moving so fast that it was impossible to slow down, and so, before she could veer off the path, her horn stabbed into the tree and stuck there. She pulled and tugged and kicked but could not dislodge herself, and so the lion, with sharp claws and teeth, tore at the unicorn's flesh and killed her. And with the tip of the unicorn's horn still stuck in the tree, the lion feasted upon her carcass.

After the unification of Scotland and England, although resentment persisted, the violence and border clashes gradually diminished. The two countries, like the lion and the unicorn who support the coat of arms, were caught in an uneasy bond. The enmity between them began to fade but it could not be completely forgotten and can still be found today.

A Persian bas-relief from the Palace of Forty Pillars in Persepolis. The story of the lion and a one-horned beast, illustrated in this frieze, appears in Babylonian seals, Mycenean coins, and other early artifacts.

VII

THE UNICORN, WILD PEOPLE AND WOOD NYMPHS

Once when he was very young, the future Charles VI of France fell upon the ground in a fit and saw the wild people riding through the woods upon their unicorns. Their bodies were almost entirely covered with hair and, except for wreaths of ferns and leaves worn around their heads, they were completely naked. Because he had often heard of the wild people and knew something about their ways, Charles was not surprised by their appearance. But the sight of the unicorns, looking as much like clouds as animals, amazed him, and he thought about them for a long time afterwards.

In 1380, when he was twelve years old, Charles became king. He still sought the wild people and the unicorns. Alone or accompanied, he wandered as far into the forests as he could. But the wild people, like the unicorns, shunned human contact, and he was never able to find them. He studied their habits and asked his tutors many questions about them. Thus he knew not to seek them on sunny days, when they would hide in

Wild Woman with Unicorn, *a tapestry chairback cover from the Upper Rhine made about 1500. The woman's body is covered with hair.*

the shadows, but during thunderstorms and blizzards when the wild people would dance in the clearings and sing guttural songs. He left acorns and berries and raw meat when he could get it, but he was not able to attract them to him.

Gradually, the thought of the wild people and the unicorns became an obsession. The beginning years of his reign were not good ones. Immediately after becoming king, upon the advice of his uncle, the duke of Anjou, Charles reinstated some taxes that had been abolished by his father, the previous monarch. Throughout France people rose up in revolt. With the count of Flanders, Charles marched against the Flemings at Roosebeke in 1382 and won a glorious victory. But rebellions broke out elsewhere, and Charles responded with fines and executions.

In 1385 when Charles announced his intention to marry Elizabeth of Bavaria, his unhappy subjects made plans for a charivari — a raucous interruption of the wedding feast. On the wedding day the castle gates were thrown open to allow everyone to celebrate the marriage. It was easy for the peasants who intended to participate in the charivari to sneak in unnoticed. They rode in through the gates wearing long cloaks and blankets. Once inside, they gathered together and threw off their wraps.

Some of them were naked; others were disguised as animals, wearing horns, masks, and skins. The leader was an enormous man dressed in green garments and green leaves. With him was a young boy, naked, who wore a unicorn mask. They serenaded the royal couple, swaying together drunkenly, singing lewd songs and making obscene noises. They jumped upon each others' backs and spread out through the crowd, dancing grotesquely around the royal guests. Their antics were frightening, and many of the guests ran off, but Charles, fascinated, watched to the very end. They looked like the wild people he had seen years before, and although he knew

Late fifteenth-century pen-and-ink drawing of a naked woman with a unicorn.

A wild person, clad only in a covering of leaves and a crown of ferns, rides a unicorn. Fifteenth century.

they were not the *true* wild people, he thought that this might be one way to bring the wild people to him.

Charles began his search then in earnest. For miles around, the castle was ringed with raw meat to attract the wild people, and young virgins were posted in forest areas throughout France in hopes that one of them would draw a unicorn. All his efforts seemed to be in vain, however, until, in 1392, a lady-in-waiting announced her marriage, and a nobleman from Normandy, who had never been fond of her, suggested a charivari. Charles decided to participate.

At the wedding drums and cymbals punctuated the drunken songs and wine was spattered over everyone. Torches smoked darkly in the corners, occasionally flaring orange. A pig had been roasted over a spit, and the guests tore at it with bare hands, while the mummers, who wandered throughout the hall, imitated every sort of animal imaginable.

Fourteenth-century miniature in Life of St. Anthony Abbot. *Note demons in upper right-hand corner. The unicorn, along with the other animals, represents the forces of evil and temptation.*

Early fifteenth-century tapestry from Upper Rhine. Wild men are shown with the unicorn, the dragon, and the lion.

In another part of the castle, in a small room far from the festivities, Charles and five of his nobles were preparing for their charivari. They donned close-fitting leggings and jerkins of fur, and they covered their heads with crowns made of horses' hair. Then the six of them chained themselves together and danced out into the celebration. They swayed this way and that, they puffed their cheeks out and made strange sounds, they rubbed up against many of the guests — both men and women — and they drank vast quantities of wine. It was immediately after he had taken a swig of juniper-flavored wine and dashed the goblet to the floor that Charles noticed there were now seven wild men, not six. He counted again to be sure, and his chest was filled with happiness, for, in the midst of the dancing and the drinking and the noise, he realized that at last a wild man had come to him. He began to shake with anticipation. The men danced around the room faster and faster, and the chains were clanging, and the songs became rowdier and rowdier.

Some of the guests ran away in fright; others drew closer to observe the antics. One guest, a young serf who worked within the castle, was surprised to see that one of the wild men in the charivari bore a close resemblance to the king. Although he had more than once been sent out to place still-warm meat around the castle and thought the king somewhat peculiar, it seemed unlikely that the king would join this devilish procession. To make sure, he drew closer.

He picked up a torch so that he could see more clearly when the men snaked by him. After a few minutes they turned in his direction. The serf held the flame closer, and as he did, one of the men lurched unexpectedly and brushed against the torch.

His fur costume caught fire at once. The acrid smell of burnt hair mingled with the smell of the roast pork, and the man on fire was screaming. The other men, chained together, began to pull in all directions. Within minutes the flames had spread to them too. The guests stopped whatever they were doing and gathered in a circle around the burning men. A few rushed forward with basins of water or jugs of wine to toss over the disguised noblemen, but their screams continued to echo clamorously and their skins bubbled. The duchess of Berry happened to be standing close to the servant with the torch and saw that one of the wild men was the king; she ran forward and

threw her velvet robe over him to smother the flames.

Although he was injured Charles lived. The other men all perished in the wedding fire. No one ever believed him when he tried to tell them about the wild man he had seen, so briefly, while he danced. Charles's mutterings became increasingly strange. From the battlements atop the castle he watched the horizon continually for a wild man on a unicorn, and for days at a time he would sneak into the woods in his wild man costume. Finally everyone realized that Charles was no longer capable of ruling. Philip the Bold of Burgundy and Louis of Orleans competed for power in his stead, and although Charles lived for another thirty years, he never governed again, and he never saw a unicorn.

During the quattrocento of the Italian Renaissance the poet Luca Pulci, who often collaborated with his brother Luigi, was in danger of losing his family estate. Attempts to save the land had met with failure until finally Luca prevailed upon his brother to help him. Luigi traveled south to Florence and explained the problem to Lorenzo de Medici, who immediately redeemed the estate.

From then on Luigi and Lorenzo were great friends. They often caroused till dawn, and Luigi's wit made him a popular member of the court. Luigi expressed his philosophy simply: "I believe no more in black than in white," he said. "But I believe in boiled or roasted capon, and I also believe in butter and beer."

Luca was different. He enjoyed writing the mock epics that Luigi favored, and he was just as glad to write in Italian rather than Latin, for it was easier. But Luigi was known as the tavern poet while Luca, who spent much of his time on his land in the hills of the Mugello, still cherished the classics. When, to everyone's surprise, Luca ran afoul of the law, even Lorenzo could not get him out of jail. Luca made repeated appeals for release. None succeeded, and he spent his last days in a stone cell.

His poetry, while not as well known as his brother Luigi's, is still remembered. A tale in one of his poems tells the story of the man who became a unicorn.

A series of engravings by Jean Duvet made about 1562 illustrating the hunt of the unicorn. In these two engravings, the unicorn purifies the river and then gores a hunter.

His name was Severe. He had spent the morning hunting and his arrows were wet with the blood of the pheasants that he carried in a bag slung over his shoulder. He was ambling rather slowly back to the small cottage where he lived in the green shade of a valley when he noticed some movements ahead of him by the lake. He hurried ahead; perhaps he would sight a stag after all. Crouching behind a large rock he peered over it toward the lake and saw three wood nymphs filling a large clay urn with water. They wore garments the color of mist, and each had a bow and a quiver full of arrows at her waist. One of the nymphs was as brown as topaz; one was the color of pink marble; and one shone like copper, or oranges, or newly minted coins.

Severe was transfixed. Ducks bobbed on the surface of the lake, and the mirror fins of fish glinted underwater. The three nymphs were dipping the urn in the water, and as they did this they splashed each other occasionally and they sang three separate songs that melded together into one. Severe had never heard anything so lovely. He dropped his bag and stood up to see them better. The one with the copper-colored skin, who was lifting the urn from the water, saw him immediately. She stopped singing, stood up with the half-filled urn clasped in her arms, and stared. He felt that he was looking at the sun, and when she and her companions turned from him and ran, her after-image burned blue in his eyes.

Chasing the three wood nymphs he could see the flashing colors of their arms and legs through the trees in front of him, but they ran more swiftly and more silently than he did. He followed them over a large outcropping of rock. When he reached the bottom, the nymphs were nowhere to be seen. Instead, in a clearing beyond the rock, he saw three trees: a tall evergreen with the wind whirring through it, a blossoming magnolia, and a maple tree with golden leaves.

Detail on a fourteenth-century Italian miniature.

He ran to the maple and threw his arms around it. His tears fell, and when at last he wiped his eyes he saw that the bark too was wet. He put his mouth to the glistening sap upon the rough bark; its sweetness exploded inside his mouth, and he forgot all about his lonely life in the cottage in the valley.

From then on Severe lived in the woods. When the sun shone in the sky he lay in the shade of the maple tree. At dusk he waited by the lake for the three nymphs to come with their urn for water. He carved a simple flute from a reed, and when he played for them, the copper-colored nymph danced in the water. At night, when the moon was high, he went hunting with them and carried back their prey for them. Occasionally the copper-colored nymph spoke to him in a low voice. He learned that her name was Nephele and that, although she looked as young as dawn, she was as old as the tree she sometimes inhabited. Severe and Nephele loved each other very much, but when he asked her to go with him to the land beyond the valley, she refused. It was her task, she said, to stay with her sisters and to fill the urn with water every day.

But the next day, when he waited by the lake at sunset, the three nymphs did not appear. Afraid he might never see them again, he fell to his knees to pray. Then, although he was very anxious, he somehow drifted into sleep. When he awoke the goddess Diana was standing above him, and she was angry. "It is forbidden," she said, "for a mortal to love a wood nymph." And with that, she reached down to the lake and splashed water in his face.

As in a dream, he felt himself changing. His neck grew longer, his arms became his forelegs, his face lengthened, a tail sprouted from the base of his spine, and from his forehead grew a single horn. Horrified, he sprang away from Diana and was amazed at the speed and agility with which he could run. The air was filled with a thousand scents he had never noticed, and he could hear the voices of the animals who burrowed beneath the ground. He felt more a part of the life of the forest than he ever had before. Just to see how it felt, he tossed his mane, switched his tail, and reared up on his hind legs. His muscles moved perfectly, and through every pore he could feel the cool forest air. He hastened to the lake, eager to have a look at himself.

At the shore he stepped carefully forward. In the still, emerald waters, he saw his reflection; he saw how beautiful he was, and he was thankful for this wonderful new life. He stared into the water, and on another part of the lake, saw the reflection of the three wood nymphs. The sound of their breathing was like the distant ocean, and when he looked up at them, Nephele was as golden as the orioles in the berry bushes, and her eyes shone amber. How he would love to ride through the forest with Nephele upon his back! He trotted toward her, and as he did, she reached into her quiver, pulled out an arrow trimmed with eagle feathers, and took aim. Severe wondered what she was aiming at, and he turned his head to survey the forest. He heard the soft creak of the wood as she pulled the bowstring back, and he heard her hold her breath, and he heard the high buzz of the string as she loosed the arrow. He looked back at her; she was the color of flame, and he saw that the arrow was aimed at him. "Nephele!" he cried, but his voice sounded entirely unlike himself, and before he could say another word, he felt the arrow pierce his smooth pale hide and then his beating heart.

He fell forward toward the water, and his legs gave way under him. He felt the water lapping at his face, and he felt the tears flow from his eyes as the blood flowed from his heart. The tears and the blood together flowed into the lake, and they kept on flowing until even his bones had turned to water and he felt his body turn to tears. The tears overflowed the boundaries of the lake and formed a river that ran through the valley and beyond; and every autumn, when Nephele wept for her lover who had disappeared, the golden leaves of the maple fell from the branches and they floated on the river to the sea.

Procris and the Unicorn *by Bernardino Luini (ca. 1475–ca. 1532). Like the man who became a unicorn and was accidentally killed by his lover, Procris was killed by her husband when he heard her moving in the trees and mistook her for an animal.*

VIII
THE MAGICAL HORN

When Moses led the children of Israel out of Egypt, they wandered in the desert for many days. They were hot and tired, and their lips were cracked. When they reached the River Marah, many people began to scoop up water in their hands to quench their thirst. But the water was so bitter that they had to spit it out. Then Moses stirred the water with his staff and it became sweet enough to drink.

In 1389 John of Hesse visited this same river and discovered that, after sunset, snakes and serpents still loosed their venom into the water so that other animals could not drink. One morning at dawn, when he happened to be walking near the river, he saw a unicorn silently dip its horn into the water to purify it. Then the other animals gathered around and drank their fill.

It was not difficult to see that, if the unicorn could cleanse the river of impurities, it might also be possible for the one-horned creature to detoxify other substances. St. Hildegard of Bingen, who lived during the twelfth century, had known of

Lady with a Unicorn
by Raphael (1483–1520).

several ways in which this ability to purify could be used for the benefit of humanity. Shoes made of unicorn hide would assure healthy legs and feet. A belt crafted of unicorn leather could keep away fevers and the plague. And unicorn liver, ground up and mashed with egg yolks, was known to be a cure for leprosy (assuming, that is, that God did not intend the patient to die).

But by far the most useful part of the unicorn was the horn. Unicorn's horn—or alicorn—was valuable as a cure against a range of maladies, and chief amongst these was the scourge of poison.

As early as the fourth century B.C. the ability of alicorn to neutralize poisons was well known. The Greek physician Ctesias wrote that water or wine which has stood for some time in a beaker made

Fifteenth-century Italian border illumination from the Bible of Borso d'Este, who chose the unicorn dipping its horn in the water as his heraldic device. Murder by poison was a common and much-feared crime during his time, and the ability of the unicorn to neutralize poison made it an attractive symbol.

of alicorn is an excellent antidote to poisons and infections of all kinds. Unfortunately this method was available only to the wealthy, for the price of unicorn horn was prohibitively high. Poor people had to make do with small quantities of horn. Perhaps a single band of the horn would be worked into a metal cup, or shavings might be ground up and used as powders. In any case, the effectiveness of alicorn was such that the smallest morsel was treasured. It was useful in protecting people against plague, fever, rabies, colic, and cramps. Boiled in wine, it whitened teeth. Mixed with amber, ivory, gold, coral, raisins, and cinnamon, it helped cure epilepsy. It is not surprising that the Apothecaries Society of London, founded in 1617, chose a pair of unicorns to support its coat of arms. The symbol was easily understood.

But as so often happens, excellence produces imitators. Merchants anxious to make a profit often sold the horns of other animals as alicorn. It became necessary to find some way to distinguish between true horn and false.

It stood to reason that true horn would possess certain properties that false horn lacked. The most notable of these attributes was the ability to detect and neutralize poisons. Several procedures were developed to verify the source of a horn. One of these involved taking a beaker carved of the horn and inverting it over two scorpions. If the scorpions died, the material was unicorn horn. If, on the other hand, the scorpions lived, the beaker was fashioned from some other substance.

If scorpions were unavailable a similar test could be performed with doves. Two doves would each be given arsenic. Then one of the doves would be fed a brew of powdered horn—and if the horn were unicorn, that bird would live. If not, both died.

James I of England, who brought the Scottish unicorn to England with him when he became king of both countries, had occasion to check the pedigree of an expensive horn he had purchased. It was important, he felt, to test his new possession, though he felt not the slightest doubt that it was indeed alicorn. James summoned a favorite servant and instructed him to drink a draught of poison to which powdered horn had been added. The servant did so, and James could not have been more

An advertisement used by a seventeenth-century London physician. King's evil and melancholy were among the diseases the horn could cure.

UNICORNS HORN

Now brought in Use for the Cure of Diseases by an Experienced DOCTOR, the AUTHOR of this Antidote.

A Most Excellent Drink made with a true *Unicorns Horn*, which doth Effectually Cure these Diseases:

Further, If any please to be satisfied, they may come to the Doctor and view the *Horn*, Viz.

- Scurvy, Old Ulcers,
- Dropsie,
- Running Gout,
- Consumptions, Distillations, Coughs
- Palpitation of the Heart,
- Fainting Fits, Convulsions,
- Kings Evil, Rickets in Children,
- Melancholly or Sadness,
- The Green Sickness, Obstructions,

And all Distempers proceeding from a Cold Cause.

The Use of it is so profitable, that it prevents Diseases and Infection by fortifying the Noble Parts, and powerfully expels what is an Enemy to Nature, preserving the Vigour, Youth, and a good Complexion to Old Age: The Virtue is of such force, as to resist an Injury from an unsound Bedfellow; None can excel this, for it is joyned with the Virtue of a true *Unicorns Horn*, through which the Drink passeth, and being impregnated therewith, it doth wonderfully Corroborate and Cure, drinking it warm at any time of the Day, about a quarter of a Pint at a time, the oftner the better, the Price is 2 s. the Quart.

2. Also as a preparative for this excellent Drink, and good against the Diseases above mentioned, and all Crudities in the Body, is ready prepared twelve Pils in a Box to be taken at three Doses, according to Directions therewith given, the Price is 2 s. the Box.

3. Likewise he hath Admirable Medicines for the Cure of the POX, or Running of the Reins, with all Simptoms and Accidents thereto belonging, whether Newly taken or of long Continuance, and (by God's Blessing) secures the Patient from the danger of the Disease presently, and perfects the Cure with the greatest Speed and Secresie imaginable, not hindering Occasions, or going abroad: Whosoever makes Use of these Admirable Medicines, may have further Advice from the Doctor without Charge.

The Doctor Liveth in Hounsditch, *next Door to* Gun-Yard, *having a Back Door into the Yard, where any Patient may come pri*

*Fifteenth-century woodcut
from* Hortus Sanitatis.

*Eighteenth-century
Spanish woodcut.*

unpleasantly surprised than when the servant promptly expired. The king had been deceived.

The only sure way to secure true horn was to take it directly from a unicorn. In the fourteenth century, when disease decimated a small Russian village, the townspeople decided to do just that.

On the barren steppes of the Crimea the summer of 1347 had been even hotter than usual. The narrow streets of the town were clogged with clouds of dust, and everyone went about with wet handkerchiefs held over their mouths. In the shops leather, stretched upon wooden frames to dry, was coated with dust, and shopkeepers swatted flies all day. Inside the huts a film lay over everything, and babies, veiled in dust, looked gray. Although a deep blue lake was within sight of the village it was too salty to drink, and other water was scarce. Several wells had already run dry. By August the ropes had to be lowered very deep into the remaining wells before the hollow thud of the bucket against the still surface of the water echoed up the dark walls. Already some of the residents of the village had started to talk about rationing water; its primary purpose, they said, had to be drinking, not washing. And so the dust sifted over everything, and tempers were short.

Thus no one really noticed anything amiss when typhoid struck. Discomfort, restlessness, heat—these sensations were normal under the circumstances. Headaches and feverishness seemed little to worry about compared to the question of when it would rain. But then Sonya, the carpenter's wife, while she was cooling her husband's feverish skin with a cloth dipped in a tiny quantity of water, noticed a spattering of oval spots of a delicate rose color across his chest. Within a few days she saw the same spots across the backs of two of her children. Shortly afterward her neighbor Anna confided that her daughter, who was soon to be married, was covered with the rosy spots and suffering from diarrhea.

At the well where the women gathered every day they learned that Anna's husband, Vasily the shepherd, was sick with the fever, and that Anna's sister-in-law was unable to go to the well herself and had to send her daughter in her stead. The women burned fires all around their cottages, and they hung herbs in the doorways, but the number of those stricken with the fever continued to rise.

Two weeks after Sonya had first noticed her husband's spots she herself was in bed. She shivered and sweated, and her legs jerked so continuously that Anna, who came to help, had to wrap the sheets aound her repeatedly. Nothing seemed to help; Sonya's tongue turned brown and dry, and although Anna fed her as much water flavored with anise and mint as she could, Sonya's tremors worsened until one morning she screamed horribly, clutched her stomach and began to talk insanely.

An hour later she was dead.

After that the fever raced through the village. The children fell sick first; when the blood ran from their noses, they died. Men groaned upon their beds and the wives, who often were just as ill, struggled to tend the sick and to fetch water from the well. At the well in the morning those few who were still strong enough to carry water through the dusty streets talked sadly about what might be done. They discussed the possibility of curing the disease with fire, with tansy, or with prayer. One woman suggested feeding the sick only with water which had

An Allegory of Chastity *by Giorgione (ca. 1478–1511).*

been boiled for several hours under the full moon. Another woman, who thought that bathing in salty sea water might help, was silenced by the blacksmith's wife, who thought bathing the very thing not to do in such a case. The women were divided on the question of a cure, and their daily discussions became sadder and more desperate.

The men—those few still strong enough to gather in the shops during the afternoons—were also worried, and one morning a few of them ventured down to the well to consult with the women. Everyone's family had been afflicted, and the discussion was heated but without resolution. At last Mikhail, whose wife and mother were both ill, suggested that the sickness could be cured if they had a unicorn horn.

Carved unicorn with narwhal tusk used as a sign for a German apothecary shop.

Some scoffed; no unicorn had ever been seen on the high steppes. But all the people of the town had heard of the miraculous powers of the unicorn, and especially of its horn. They agreed it would be worth a try. Everyone knew how to catch a unicorn; it was common knowledge that a unicorn could be captured only by a virgin. And that, they suddenly realized, was a problem. For although everyone thought and thought, they could not think of a single virgin in the town. Many, including Anna's daughter, had died of the disease. Other girls were dreadfully sick. The townspeople remembered with frustration that only a few days before several young girls, and several infants as well, had been sent in a wooden cart to a distant village to the north in order to escape the disease. A few spinsters lived in the town, but the women felt that they had chosen their way for reasons other than lack of opportunity—and one man, perhaps not the most trustworthy, confirmed that supposition. The unicorn's slightest doubt about the woman would be enough to jeopardize the plan, for it was thought that it would kill any woman who falsely claimed to be a virgin.

The women with their water buckets walked back home. The men also scattered. The next morning at the well the women talked among themselves, lamenting the punishment that had come to the village and lamenting the lack of a virgin. They were taken aback, then, when Katya, normally so quiet, volunteered to try to capture the unicorn. Some of the women started to laugh, for Katya, with several children of uncertain lineage, was a notorious non-virgin. But the grave look on her wide face and the seriousness of the situation silenced them. Katya outlined her plan. She would be willing to try to attract the unicorn, she said, but only under one condition: that the men not be informed of the plan until after the unicorn had purged the town of disease and been released. At first her idea was greeted with skepticism, but gradually the women accepted it. Perhaps the unicorn would be fooled, or perhaps the unicorn would come despite the lack of a virgin. The worst that could happen would be that the unicorn would kill Katya, and truthfully, they said to each other, with four small children sick at home she might die anyway. Two of the women vowed that, should something happen to Katya, they would care for her children. Then they rushed home to deposit their water-filled buckets and returned to the well.

Katya was already there in her Sunday clothes which, although they were patched, were at least somewhat clean. With the other women in a silent column behind her, she walked past the walls of the town and toward the saline lake. At the shore, she sat down upon a smooth stone, folded her hands in her lap, and waited. The other women stayed some distance apart, where those with sharp vision could just barely see her and those with fine hearing could hear her soft song. They waited for a long time. But everyone knew how important it was that the unicorn come, and everyone concentrated hard on that thought. And their efforts succeeded. At last, in the late afternoon, the unicorn trotted lightly across the flat plain of the

Girl with Unicorn, *painted about 1450 by an unknown artist.*

steppe and approached Katya.

When it was almost close enough for her to reach out and touch, the unicorn stopped. With its eyes fixed on her face, it took a halting step backward. For her part, Katya gazed steadfastly at the unicorn and tried not to be afraid. A full minute passed while Katya and the unicorn looked at each other. Far away, the other women could hear that her song had ceased, and they could see that the unicorn had not yet yielded to her. They held their breaths, and finally the unicorn hesitantly stepped forward and put its head in Katya's lap, where she stroked it and held its horn.

They stayed that way for a long time, until the women got tired of waiting and went back home to their families. Then, when she was alone with the unicorn, Katya stood up, wrapped a long strip of linen around the unicorn's neck, and led it into town. At each well they stopped and Katya hauled up a bucket of water. The unicorn dipped its horn into the water. Water that was slightly muddy or a little green bubbled for a moment until it looked as though it were boiling. Then it became as clear as air, and she lowered it back into the well. When the pure water splashed into the dingy well, she heard the sounds of effervescence and felt the tiny

bubbles on her face. In this way the unicorn purified the water in each of the wells.

The sun had set. Throughout the village only a few candles were flickering when Katya and the unicorn began to stop at the houses. The unicorn dipped its horn into each basin; and water that had been discolored, that had specks of dirt floating on top—water that had already been used several times to wash—became clear. The people of the town marveled. The unicorn would allow only Katya to come near; but some of the people began to follow behind them, and a few held their children in their arms and told them to watch and remember. Wherever people were particularly ill the unicorn held its horn a few inches above their bodies, and they began to feel better at once. In those homes the women cried their thanksgiving and some of them followed the unicorn; some of the men were curious too and joined the hushed procession. All night Katya and the unicorn moved through the town. By dawn every drop of water had been purified, and everyone who had been sick felt better. At sunup Katya and the unicorn

Paintings by Susan Boulet.

stood again at the well. She leaned toward the unicorn to untie the linen strip and set it free.

By then a considerable group of people had gathered behind her. Among them were some of the men from the town. They had watched with amazement as the unicorn purified the water and healed the people, and they were grateful to Katya for risking her life to bring the unicorn to them. But at the same time they could not help but think about the future. What if another epidemic came to the town? What would happen then?

And it occurred to one of the men, who spoke his mind to the others, that if they had the unicorn-horn here in the town they would be safe in the future as well.

And then another man proposed a different idea. Unicorn horn, he said, was worth a great deal of money. They could bring it to the shore, where ships came to trade, and sell it for a goodly sum. His idea met with much praise. One man said that he was certain another such epidemic would never come to the town, for the unicorn had already purified all the water. Another said that with the money they could gain by selling the horn, they could always buy a unicorn goblet for future emergencies. The men were all impressed with these thoughts. So when they saw Katya untying the linen leash about the unicorn's neck, they called her name. She stopped what she was doing and looked up. Perhaps, she thought, a house had been neglected, or maybe they had forgotten a tiny pond or an old well. But still she held on to the leash and the unicorn, who had been docile the whole time, began to paw the ground and pull away from her. Suddenly one of the men leaped forward and grabbed Katya, pulling her away. She screamed. The unicorn dashed forward and speared the man through the belly with its horn; and as the man screamed, and Katya screamed, and the other women drew away in horror, the men swarmed around the unicorn and slew it.

Although the men tried to explain their reasoning to Katya, she was inconsolable and ran back to her children. She poured the water that the unicorn had purified into a stoppered bottle, packed up a few odds and ends—her mother's samovar, a length of patterned cloth, a rough bowl and cup—and loaded her children into the wagon. She would find another town, she thought; she could no

longer live here. A few of the women tried to argue with her, to convince her to stay, but she would not change her mind. With her children she rode back toward the open steppe where she had first met the unicorn.

The men, meanwhile, were busy. They had removed the horn and were skinning the unicorn now, trying to preserve as many of its parts as they could for possible sale. When they had at last completed their work and the dusty road where they had killed the unicorn was black with blood, they loaded the parts into a cart and covered it with straw. Then one of the men—Sergius, the tanner—drove the cart to market.

He rode to a prosperous seaside town that overlooked the Black Sea, and when he arrived he was happy to hear that a ship had just pulled into port for trading. He was a wily businessman; he drove the straw-covered cart down to the shore and bargained with the merchants on board. He did well, and when he returned to the cart, he was glad that it was still covered with straw, for he had many bags of gold to carry as well as several large crates of sweet oranges, three sacks of sugar, and a wooden box full of fragrant spices from the East.

He covered everything with the straw, and as he was doing this, he considered the possibility of disappearing with the gold. He might, for example, simply get on a ship and sail to another port. He thought about riding to another village too. But then he remembered his life in the little town, and his family; and he felt that the wealth really belonged to everyone, with perhaps an extra coin or two for Katya, who, after all, had risked her life. He drove back to the village.

When he arrived, the men were waiting for him. They unloaded the sacks of gold anxiously, and everyone began to bicker about the best way to divide the gold. Some claimed that every family should be given an equal amount. Others—the men with large families—thought that the amount of gold should depend upon the number of children. Those with invalids in the family should receive an extra stipend, said some men. Those who never married deserved less, said others. The bickering went on far into the night.

And so it was that, while they looked at the piles of gold, no one noticed that three or four rats, who had gnawed their way into the orange crates on the ship, slipped out between the slats and scurried away.

A few weeks later, the rats had multiplied and several citizens of the town began to feel poorly. They were delirious, and had to hide their eyes from the sun. Their heads throbbed unmercifully. Their tongues began to swell and turned white. Then they noticed in their groins and under their arms the dark swollen tokens of the black plague. The pestilence swept through the village, and no one connected it with their betrayal of the unicorn.

Virgin and unicorn,
from an early fourteenth-century tapestry
illustrating feminine wiles.

PART THREE

THE
PROGRESS OF THE
UNICORN

IX

CENTURIES OF SEARCH

During the twelfth century, when thousands of people were dying in unsuccessful crusades, a curious story arose about a fabulous king who lived in Asia and was known as Prester John. He had fought victoriously, it was said, against the kings of Persia and had afterwards attempted to conquer Jerusalem. However, his journey to that city was cut short when he arrived at the Tigris River and was unable to cross. He headed north, for he had heard that the river there was frozen solid and his troops could easily walk over it. This information proved false; he waited several years for the river to freeze and finally, after losing many men as a result of the poor conditions, he was forced to return to India.

Twenty years later he wrote a letter to Emanuel, emperor of Constantinople. In it he described himself as a devout Christian and as the greatest ruler on earth. It was reassuring to the Europeans, whose lives had been buffeted by a half-century of futile crusades attempting to wrest Jerusalem from the hands of the Moslems, to discover the existence of a

Detail of The Parliament of Beasts *from* Bartholomew the Englishman's De Proprietatibus rerum, *about 1480.*

great Christian empire that had, evidently, resolved many of the problems still plaguing their own. Prester John's empire, for instance, had eradicated poverty, and, more remarkable still, it had eliminated thievery, flattery, miserliness, lies and all vice — although cannibalism was occasionally practiced.

Prester John's kingly trappings were very grand. The palace roof was made of ebony, the floor of onyx, and the windows of crystal. When he went to war his men carried fourteen gold crosses instead of banners. His empire was enormous, with seventy-two separate kingdoms under his rule. Despite the size of his realm Prester John was able to know everything that was happening in it simply by gazing in a special mirror mounted on a pedestal many stories high. He was attended by a multitude of people with important titles: kings, dukes, counts, archbishops and bishops; even his chief cook was an abbot and king. But John himself, out of modesty, chose only the humble title prester, or presbyter, meaning priest or elder.

The kingdom was also filled with miracles of nature. "Our land streams with honey and is overflowing with milk," he wrote. "In one region grows no poisonous herb, nor does a querulous frog ever quack in it; no scorpion exists, nor does the serpent glide amongst the grass, nor can any poisonous animals exist in it, or injure anyone." Those who drank three times from a certain bubbling stream would always be as healthy as they had been at thirty, no matter how long they might live. Anyone who looked at a certain stone could be sure of having excellent vision, while those who stepped into a particular fountain — assuming they first were willing to state that they were Christians or planned to convert — were purged of all past sins and illnesses.

A strange river, made entirely of stone, ran along the outskirts of the kingdom. It could not be crossed when the rocks were rolling and crashing to the sea. Fortunately, however, it stopped flowing four days a week and then it was possible to cross it. Beyond this river of stone lived the ten tribes of the Jews, who were slaves to the king.

All of this was good news to the Christians of Europe, and indeed, after Prester John's famous letter — and copies of it — had circulated for some time, Pope Alexander III sent a reply. His

Twelfth-century miniature from Physiologus *manuscript. According to Aelian (ca. 170–235), "In certain regions of India . . . they say there are impassable mountains full of wild life. . . . And in these same regions there is said to exist a one-horned beast."*

message was a cautious one; he greeted John as a brother in Christ, and he warned against a boastful spirit. From that time on, the rulers of Europe were interested in establishing contact with Prester John, while those who had traveled to Asia tried to link his name with those of known rulers there.

Their efforts, however, were in vain, and by the fourteenth century the public imagination had definitely moved Prester John's court from the plains of India to the mountains of Abyssinia (in what is now Ethiopia). That this should occur is not as puzzling as it might seem, for during the Middle Ages India and Abyssinia were much confused.

With the move to Africa, Prester John began to receive European visitors; their reports, filtering back, confirmed what people had thought about that wonderful place. Prester John in his original letter had catalogued some of the inhabitants of his realm, and the list was a miraculous one:

Our land is the home of elephants, dromedaries, camels, crocodiles, meta-collinarum, cametennus, tensevetes, wild asses, white and red lions, white bears, white merles, crickets, griffins, tigers, lamias, hyaenas, wild horses, wild oxen and wild men, men with horns, one-eyed, men with eyes before and behind, centaurs, fauns, satyrs, pygmies, forty-ell high giants, Cyclopses, and similar women; it is the home too of the phoenix, and of nearly all living animals.

Although he did not mention the unicorn, it came as a surprise to no one to learn that the unicorn, too, inhabited that wonderful realm. Edward Webbe, an Elizabethan adventurer and the author of a book entitled *The Rare and most wonderful thinges which Edward Webbe has seen,* wrote about the unicorns there: "I have seen in a place like a park adjoyning unto prester Iohn's Court, three score and seven-teene unicornes and eliphants all alive at one time, and they were so tame that I have played with them as one would play with young Lambes."

Nor was Webbe the only one to describe the unicorns from Prester John's court. John Bermudez, who visited Ethiopia in 1535, reported that the unicorns there were very fierce and large and shaped like horses. Another man, called Marmolius, said the unicorn that lived "among the Mountains of the Moon in High Ethiopia" was as large as a two-year-old colt, with a beard and a grooved horn. Other travelers, who were unable

The unicorn with other wild beasts.

A variety of unicorn, the camphur has as its most unusual feature not its horn but its feet, which resemble those of a cow in front and those of a bird in back

to reach Prester John's court, were fortunate in being able to visit monarchs who had received gifts of unicorns from him. Louys Paradis, a Parisian doctor, saw such an animal in Alexandria, although clearly it was not the same sort of unicorn that other people had described. The creature Paradis saw was the size of a large hunting dog, with a dark coat, a dark horn about a foot long, and one yellow forefoot. Its favorite food was sugarcane. Nonetheless, this animal provided another piece of evidence attesting to the happy existence of a multitude of unicorns in the kingdom of Prester John.

Fifteenth-century miniature from the Livre des Merveilles.

OPPOSITE
Various unicorns, from Peter Pomet's pharmaceutical text, Histoire des Drogues, *1694.*

Throughout Europe this magical court was well-known, for it had been reported upon by many trustworthy (and otherwise) sources, including Vasco Da Gama and King John II of Portugal. By the sixteenth century — when Prester John was close to five hundred years old — a series of Christian missionaries made the journey to Ethiopia. Many of them confirmed the existence of the unicorn, but here and there a note of doubt about Prester John began to creep in. Some people admitted that "Prester John of the Indies" was simply a name for the Abyssinian emperor. And so the story of Prester John faded away, though the story of the unicorn lived on.

The unicorn was first described in the fourth century B.C. by Ctesias, a Greek physician who had heard tales from visitors to India. The animal he portrayed was quite different from the one we now picture for, among other things, it had a tri-color horn of white, black and red. His description was picked up readily by other Greeks and Romans. Aristotle commented briefly on the unicorn and so did Julius Caesar, who reported that a one-horned animal lived in the Hercynian Forest of Germany. In his *Gallic Wars* Caesar wrote, "It is known that many kinds of animals not seen in other places

breed therein. . . . There is an ox, shaped like a stag, from the middle of whose forehead, between the ears, stands forth a single horn, taller and straighter than the horns we know."

Pliny the Elder, who lived in first-century Rome, wrote about an animal called the monoceros which had feet like an elephant and a long black horn. In the third century A.D. the naturalist Aelian added to the fund of information on the unicorn. Clearly he had read his Ctesias, for he told of an animal that very much resembled the one portrayed by Ctesias—but he also described, for the first time, a slightly different beast which had spiral markings on its horn.

Most of the ancient thinkers who discussed the unicorn, including Aristotle, based their knowledge on hearsay rather than first-hand observation. One man, however, claimed he saw the unicorn. His name was Apollonius of Tyana. During the first century A.D. he journeyed from his native Greece, where he had studied the doctrines of Pythagoras, to India, where he saw the one-horned wild asses described by Ctesias and heard about the medicinal properties of the horn. The rulers of India, he was told, drank from cups made of the horn as protection against sickness and poison. Yet Apollonius—who was thought to have magical powers himself—was sceptical on that point. "I should have believed it," he said, "if I had found that the kings of this country were immortal."

During the Middle Ages belief in the unicorn was spread by the Bible, which mentioned it seven times, while knowledge of the unicorn—of its habits and its significance—was spread by the Physiologus, a naturalist who lived between the second and fifth centuries, possibly in Egypt, and who wrote a bestiary in Greek. Its influence was incalculable; it was translated and recopied and expanded for over a thousand years. From this book people of the Middle Ages learned about the unicorn; because of this book they commenced to search for it.

Marco Polo was one of the first explorers to mention the unicorn, but his disappointment in it was great. Expecting the fabulous beast he had heard described, he found instead the rhinoceros. He described the animals he saw on his journey to the Far East:

They have wild elephants, and great numbers of unicorns hardly smaller than elephants in size. Their hair is like that of a buffalo, and their feet like those of an elephant. In the middle of their forehead is a very large black horn. Their head is like that of a wild boar, and is always carried bent to the ground. They delight in living in mire and mud. It is a hideous beast to look at, and in no way like what we think and say in our countries, namely a beast that lets itself be taken in the lap of a virgin. Indeed, I assure you that it is altogether different from what we fancied.

Although Marco Polo obviously did not see the true unicorn, others were more fortunate. In 1389 a visitor to the Holy Land, John of Hesse, saw a unicorn dipping its horn into a river in order to purify it for the other animals. Almost a century

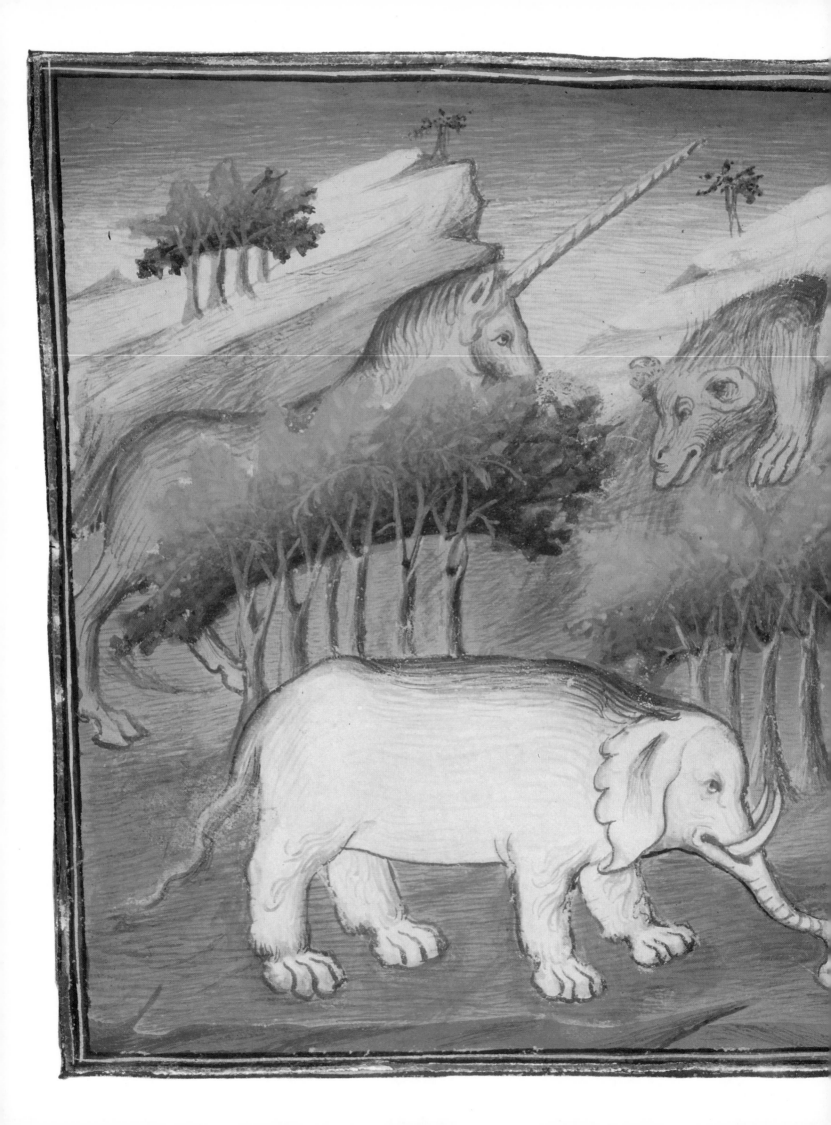

PREVIOUS PAGE
"There are wild elephants in the country, and numerous unicorns which are nearly as big," wrote Marco Polo (1254–1324). *This fifteenth-century miniature from the* **Livre des Merveilles** *illustrates some of the wonders that he saw.*

Three varieties of unicorn, by Erhard Renwick from Perigrinationes ad Terram Sanctum, *1486.*

later, Felix Fabri sighted a unicorn near Mount Sinai. In 1503 Lewis Vartoman, the author of *Itinerario*, reported on several unicorns he saw in a park in Mecca. Moreover, in Ethiopia he saw one-horned cattle in the city of Zeila—possibly they were gifts from Prester John. Other travelers during this time also saw, or heard of, the unicorn. Its existence seemed well documented.

One prominent account of a unicorn was written by Jieronymo Lobo, a seventeenth-century Portuguese missionary who spent some time in Abyssinia, where the emperor had recently been converted to Christianity by another Jesuit. After several years, however, the emperor changed his mind and banished all the Jesuits, including Lobo, who was later captured, first by Turks and then by pirates. Nonetheless he found time to write two books about Ethiopia; in both he describes sightings of the unicorn. "The country of the Unicorn (an African animal, only known there) is the Province of Agaos in the kingdom of Damotes; that it may wander into places more remote is not improbable." He then discussed various sightings and concluded that "These testimonies . . . confirms me that this so celebrated Unicorne is in this Province, there foales, and bred."

The unicorn was also observed in America. During the sixteenth century two men reported that the unicorn existed in Florida; one told of a unicorn with a curved horn and a body as big as an ox, while another claimed that not only were there unicorns in Florida (which he knew for a fact because many of the Floridians wore pieces of horn about their necks), but that the unicorn would dip its horn into the water before drinking. He pointed out that there were lions and tigers in Florida as well.

In the seventeenth century Dr. Olfert Dapper described unicorns sighted in Maine and on the Canadian border. Apparently he himself did not see the fabulous beast, but he reported upon what he had heard: "On the Canadian border, there are sometimes seen animals resembling horses, but with cloven hoofs, rough manes, a long straight horn upon the forehead, a curled tail like that of the wild boar, black eyes, and a neck like that of a stag. They live in the loneliest wilderness."

In the New World belief and interest in the unicorn never took on the proportions they had in the Old World; and even there, confidence in the creature's existence waned. During the eighteenth and nineteenth centuries travelers still published occasional accounts—usually second-hand—of unicorns seen in far-away places. Africa was the most frequently mentioned habitat, with many Europeans claiming to have heard about the animal from various native peoples. Sir Francis Galton, for instance, visited South Africa in the middle of the nineteenth century and made the following report:

The Bushmen, without any leading question or previous talk upon the subject, mentioned the unicorn. I cross-examined them thoroughly, but they persisted in describing a one-horned animal, something like a gemsbok in shape and size, whose one horn was in the middle of its forehead and pointed forwards. . . . It will be strange indeed if, after all, the creature has a real existence. There are recent travelers in the north of tropical Africa who have heard of it there, and believe in it, and there is surely plenty of room to find something new in the vast belt of *terra incognita* that lies in this continent.

Similar rumors floated out of Tibet. Nonetheless belief in the unicorn diminished. Some scholars were beginning to discuss the unicorn, not as a zoological curiosity but as a mythological one; the belief that the importance of the unicorn lay in its legend rather than in the possibility of its existence began to gather force.

Throughout its history the strength of that legend rose and fell with the times. In Western culture, although a few Greeks and Romans mentioned the unicorn, its existence did not gain a hold on the public imagination until the translation of the Bible into Greek in the third century B.C. and the compilation, several centuries later, of the bestiary by the Physiologus. By that time the unicorn existed not only as an animal with certain predictable traits and habits but as a symbol of Christ. This metaphor contributed much toward the popularity of the unicorn in the West. At various times other writers discussed the unicorn, including St. Basil in the fourth century and Isidore of Seville in the seventh. Their comments confirmed the animal's existence. Indeed, people of the Middle Ages had no more reason to doubt the existence of the unicorn than they did to doubt the existence of the elephant or the camel, which they had also never seen, and which in certain ways seemed far less likely creatures than the unicorn. And so the legend grew. By the thirteenth century the unicorn was a powerful enough figure that it was credited with altering history. One story illustrates the force the

Detail from
The Parliament of Beasts.

LEFT
*Seizure of the unicorn, from a
ninth-century* Physiologus.

BELOW
*Unicorn hunt in India. Engraved by J. Collaert after
J. van der Straet (1523–1605).*

*Woodcut from a German edition of Aesop's Fables
illustrating the dispute between four-footed and
winged beasts, about 1476.*

unicorn still possessed:

In 1224 Genghis Khan, after almost a lifetime of conquest, prepared to march into Hindustan. In the course of his sixty-two years he had conquered many lands and presided over the killing of many people. His empire stretched from Korea to the Persian Gulf. Very few had been willing to oppose him. So when he climbed the slopes of Mount Dja-danaring he anticipated little difficulty in taking over the great Indian peninsula of Hindustan. At the top of the mountain, however, he was met not by a battalion of enemy soldiers but by a single green unicorn who understood four languages. Three times the unicorn knelt at his feet, and

BELOW
This engraving by Romeyn de Hooge (ca. 1650–1720) was the frontispiece of Thomas Bartholinus's De Unicornu.

Genghis Khan, for some reason, was immediately put in mind of his father, also a conqueror, who had died almost fifty years before. Genghis Kahn was not normally a man given to introspection, but the appearance of the unicorn awed him. His troops milled about in confusion while he thought; his closest generals waited to hear his pronouncement. At last he called them together. "This middle kingdom of India before us is the place, men say, in which the sublime Buddha and the Bodhisattvas and many powerful princes were born. What may it mean that this wild animal bows before me like a man? Is it that the spirit of my father would send me a warning out of heaven?"

OPPOSITE
The unicorn and the stag were often pictured together, as in this seventeenth-century image. According to the ancient alchemists, the unicorn represented spirit while the stag represented soul.

No one could say otherwise, and so Genghis Khan turned his troops around and marched back down the mountain. Unlike so many places before, Hindustan remained unharmed, untouched by the Mongol invader, preserved by the unicorn.

By the end of the fifteenth century (when the famous tapestries were made) the unicorn had become a common artistic device; yet simultaneously its credibility as a member of the physical world began a slow decline. Voyagers to distant places continued to report its existence, but the times had changed; new worlds were being explored across the ocean, and a new spirit of rationalism and scepticism began to spread. By the beginning of the seventeenth century, when Shakespeare expressed his doubt about the unicorn and Cervantes' Don Quixote briefly considered calling himself the Knight of the Unicorn before settling on the Knight of the Doleful Countenance as his sobriquet, many people had strong doubts. Expeditions continued to sight the unicorn. People still speculated about possible places where it might live. But they also were beginning to relegate the unicorn to the archives of mythology. It was this diminished status that paved the way, in the twentieth century, for the first authenticated unicorn in history: a creature not of the imagination but of the laboratory.

Fifteenth-century miniature from the Livre des Merveilles.

X

THE FALSE UNICORN

When we think of the unicorn today a particular picture comes to mind: it must be white, shaped like a horse, with a spiraling horn the color of ivory. Basically, it should look like the animal in the famous *Hunt of the Unicorn* tapestries. We would do well to remember that many descriptions of the unicorn do not agree with this image. The Chinese k'i-lin was shaped like a small cow and covered with scales, while another Chinese unicorn had a stag's body and a dragon's head. The Japanese kirin had five different colors, the sin-you looked like a lion, and yet another Eastern unicorn had a shell like a turtle. The Arabian karkadann resembled the rhinoceros; inside the horn were carved figures of humans, peacocks and cattle. The karkadann was also portrayed as having thick unjointed legs so that it could never lie down and was forced to lean against trees. The Biblical unicorn, according to some sources, was as big as a mountain, and a unicorn of Persia had nine mouths and a horn made of gold.

Ctesias, who gave us the first written description

Detail from left wing of altarpiece by Hieronymus Bosch (1460–1516).

of a unicorn, reported that it had a white body, a red head, and blue eyes, and that the horn was white on the bottom, black in the middle and red at the tip. He also wrote that it had an exceedingly lovely ankle-bone (which was used, in later times, for making dice). Aristotle knew of several different kinds of unicorns, which he classified into two categories: those with cloven hoofs, such as the oryx, and those with solid hoofs, such as the Indian ass. Pliny the elder, writing in the first century A.D., said the unicorn had "a body like a horse, head like a stag, feet like an elephant, and tail like a boar . . . and one black horn." Aelian and many later writers (and artists) agreed with Pliny that the unicorn's body was like the horse's.

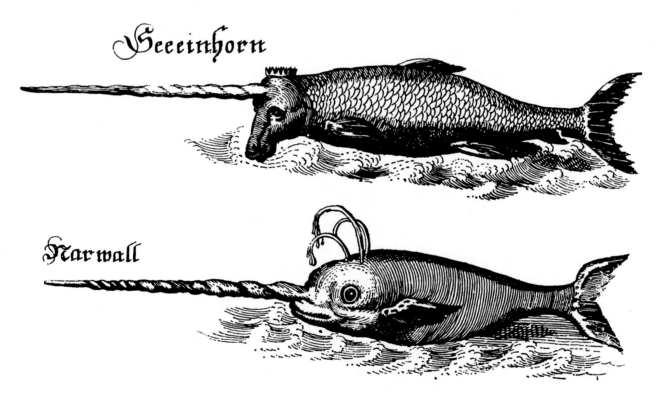

Sea unicorn and narwhal
from Peter Pomet's pharmaceutical text,
Histoire des Drogues, *1694.*

But Physiologus disagreed. His unicorn looked like a goat, with a beard and cloven hoofs; it was a small and humble animal. The slight size of the goat was often appealing, but so was the grace and beauty of the horse. The horse and the goat have merged in the image we have today, which has the body of the one and the beard of the other. But the zoological ancestors of the unicorn include far more exotic beasts than these common animals.

The most distinctive feature of the unicorn is, of course, its horn. Early commentators ascribed different colors to it, and its length was equally variable. It was also commonly held throughout the

Middle Ages that at the base of the horn was a ruby, called the carbuncle, which was imbued with magical properties, including the abilities to cure melancholy, eliminate nightmares, detect poison and protect against the plague. Eventually the carbuncle lost its significance and the practical properties became attached to the horn itself. The idea of the horn came from a variety of sources, but the image of the horn as we know it today—and have known it for over a millenium—came from one place: the upper reaches of the North Sea, where the narwhal swims in icy waters.

The narwhal is a curious animal. Swimming in small groups in the remote Arctic, it is a mammal, not a fish, and its chief value to humans stems from one feature: the male narwhal has a tooth in its jaw which juts out through its lips and grows, in a spiraling motion, as long as eight feet. This tooth, which is ivory, is exactly what we think of when we picture the unicorn's horn. Indeed, it *is* the unicorn's horn.

No one knows when the teeth of the narwhal began to circulate around Europe. We do know that by the twelfth century sailors already had them earmarked as worthwhile merchandise. In 1126 a ship went down off the coast of Iceland. Many of the bodies floated into a marsh known, several centuries later, as the Pool of Corpses. Along with those bodies were a number of long "whales' teeth" marked with runes that carefully identified the

Twelfth-century water unicorn from the painted ceiling of a Swiss church.

owner of each tusk; so even then the narwhal's tooth was worth something, a piece of property to be labeled. Throughout the Middle Ages and the Renaissance unicorn horns—narwhal teeth—were owned by the monarchs and popes of Europe. They were very valuable. King Edward I of England owned a unicorn horn (which was stolen in 1303), as did Charles VI of France. In 1553 Pope Clement gave a unicorn horn decorated with gold to Henry II, the king of France. Philip II of Spain owned twelve unicorn horns, a gift from the sultan of Turkey. Mary Queen of Scots owned a horn, as did Francis I (husband of Catherine de Medici). Frederick III of Denmark had a throne made almost entirely of narwhal tusks. Many monasteries also owned alicorns, but the most famous horn of all—known as the Horn of Windsor—belonged to Elizabeth I of England.

That particular horn came to the queen not from another monarch but directly from the man who found it, Martin Frobisher. A captain in the British navy, he had for some time been trying to discover a northwest passage to India. He was forced to turn back during his first attempt in 1576 because of rough winds and cold weather, but the trip was not a total failure. Some of his men found some "black earth" and the rumor quickly arose that it was gold. That made it much easier for him to find backers for future journeys, and the very next year he set out again. Inclement weather interfered once more with his explorations. When several ships were wrecked by a sudden storm, Frobisher came to a halt. He had made it as far as an inlet now known as Frobisher's Bay in Baffin Island, Canada. His men, who had spent most of their time there collecting ore, also found a "great dead fish" with a hollow spiraling tusk almost two yards long. During the Middle Ages and the Renaissance many people believed that for every animal of the land there was an equivalent animal of the ocean. This dead whale was clearly a sea unicorn, but just to be sure, the sailors tested the horn. Poisonous spiders, placed in the inner cavity, died. This provided adequate proof that the horn must belong to the unicorn of the sea. As an antidote to poison it was worth a great deal. Frobisher, who was later knighted for his valor against the Spanish Armada, took the horn back to Queen Elizabeth. It was reputed to be worth one hundred thousand pounds—

ABOVE AND OPPOSITE
Three details from left wing of altarpiece by Hieronymus Bosch.

a sizable sum even now.

It may be that some sailors' faith in unicorns was shaken by the discovery that the horn could be attached to a dead whale. Others perhaps accepted the existence of the sea unicorn as proof that, somewhere, there must be a land unicorn. In any case narwhal teeth provided an easy way to earn extra money for enterprising sailors of the northern seas. Certainly to those at home who had never seen the narwhal the spiraling horn was compelling evidence of the existence of the unicorn.

Despite knowledge of the narwhal people wanted to believe in the unicorn—and in the magical powers of the horn. Some people, upon being convinced that there was no such thing as the unicorn, ascribed to the tooth of the narwhal the traits of the alicorn. Many people still had great faith in the horn as an aid to health. In England, for example, unicorn horn appeared on official lists of effective medicines as late as the eighteenth century.

Still other people believed in the existence of the unicorn but placed little faith in the efficacy of the horn. Caspar Bartholinus and Thomas Browne were two men who believed in the unicorn while doubting the amazing properties of the horn. The French physician Ambroise Paré, after a series of experiments in which unicorn horn had no effect upon the behavior of scorpions, also discounted the medicinal value of the horn. His views, ignored at first, eventually were accepted. Thus, as might be expected, it was science which finally deposed the unicorn—and it was science which resurrected it.

The demise of the unicorn came about in part through the work of the French naturalist Baron

Georges Leopold Cuvier. Cuvier was a much respected scientist who, among other things, did a great deal of paleontological research and was instrumental in helping to identify several of the first dinosaur fossils to be unearthed. In 1827, some years after he had been appointed to several important positions by Napoleon, he made the announcement that an animal with cloven hoofs—and it was agreed that the unicorn was such an animal—could not, by its very structure, have a single horn. Animals with cloven hoofs, he said, would have divided frontal lobes; in order to have one horn symmetrically placed, that horn would perforce have to grow over the division in the skull—and that would be impossible. Therefore, the unicorn did not—could not—exist.

It was a mighty argument, difficult to disprove (despite the existence of the rhinoceros, which did not really count because that animal lacks a true horn; the horn of the rhinoceros actually consists of agglutinated hair). After Cuvier's statement the unicorn languished without a scientific defender. Then, surprisingly, it found a champion once more.

The time was March 1933. In Washington D.C.

Dr. Dove's unicorn at two years of age.

Franklin D. Roosevelt had just been inaugurated president of the United States. In Germany the Reichstag had voted to confer practically unlimited powers upon the recently appointed chancellor, Adolf Hitler. And at the University of Maine, Dr. W. Franklin Dove had just performed an operation turning a day-old male calf into a unicorn. He was aware of Cuvier's ideas; but Cuvier, Dove asserted, was mistaken in his ideas about where horns grow. Cuvier presumed that horns were outgrowths of the skull, whereas Dove, who was in charge of an experimental biology station, had recently proved that at least with cows this was not the case. Horns were formed separately and then rooted to the skull; they did not emerge from it.

With this in mind Dove performed a relatively simple operation. He transplanted the two horn buds (small bits of tissue that later produce horn) to the center of the skull so that they lay side by side over the frontal division of the skull. He also trimmed the horn buds, which are normally round, so that they were flat along the side where they touched, providing maximum contact. Dove's hope was that the two horn buds would fuse together and develop into a single horn. And indeed, that is what happened. The horn grew singly, short and straight, and the unicorn flourished. It was able to use its one horn profitably both in passing under fences and in attacking other animals. The horn was a natural weapon which provided the unicorn with a real advantage over others in the herd. Yet at the same time, perhaps because it was conscious of its peculiar power, it was a most gentle, even docile creature. It had more than just the horn of the unicorn; it also had something of the character of that fabled beast.

Perhaps, Dove speculated, this animal was just another of a series of artificially produced unicorns. Aelian, Pliny the Elder, and others had reported one-horned cattle living in Ethiopia. In 1796 a traveler in Africa described a method he had seen of manipulating the horns of oxen in order to produce unicorns. In 1921 a report came from Nepal of an operation in which sheep could be converted from two-horned to one-horned animals. The Dinkas, a people who lived in the southern Sudan, and the Kaffirs of South Africa also were acquainted with such artificial methods, and they used them as a way of distinguishing—or, perhaps, producing—

At fifteen months of age, the unicorn has a single horn solidly attached to the center of its skull.

OPPOSITE
St. Justine *by Moretto de Brescia (1498–1555). Although other artists of the time gave the unicorn a long, pale horn, Moretto's image is in accord with descriptions left by several ancient writers, who claimed the unicorn's horn was dark.*

 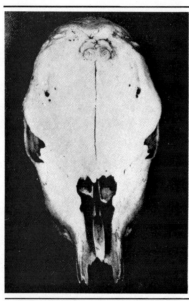

LEFT
The newly-made unicorn, immediately after the horn buds have been transplanted from the outer edges of the skull to the center.

RIGHT
The skull of a potential unicorn four months old. The horn buds, manipulated so that they lie in the center of the skull, have fused together.

the leaders of their herds. So while Dr. Dove might appear, at first glance, to be the Frankenstein of unicorns, further investigation shows that he was but one in a long line of men who made unicorns.

His unicorn, it is true, is peculiarly unromantic looking. Stolidly bovine, it lacks both mystery and grace. But any objections one might have to its unprepossessing appearance are at least somewhat defused upon greater reflection; for the Chinese k'i-lin, it will be recalled, was the size and shape of a calf (although it was admittedly also covered with dragon-like scales). The common shape of this most recent unicorn—the only one of which we have photographs—is not something new. It dates back twenty-five hundred years.

Nor is the shape the only historical parallel to Dr. Dove's unicorn. There remains the central question of the horn. The horn on Dr. Dove's unicorn, unlike the tooth of the narwhal, was white at the base and black at the tip. The unicorn of Ctesias had a horn that was white at the base, black in the middle, and red at the tip. Dove offers two possible explanations for the discrepancy. It is not uncommon, he says, for light reflected from the black tip to appear scarlet. And—if that seems far-fetched—he points out that had he used a female Ayrshire calf rather than a male, the tip of the horn would have been red, for the color difference is a sex-linked genetic trait in this particular breed. The most unlikely part of Ctesias's description—the tricolor horn—turns out, then, to be based on something other than total imagination. Suddenly stories from the past become more possible than they once seemed. Plutarch, for example, tells of a unicorn ram given to Pericles in the fifth century B.C. Later, unicorn rams from Nepal were given to the Prince of Wales in 1906, and upon examination these animals turned out to be the product of artificial manipulation of the horn buds. So Dr. Dove's method, rather than being the twentieth-century aberration it might at first appear to be, may in reality be an ancient technique used to produce a synthetic version of the most superior animal of them all: the unicorn.

XI
MYTH AND MASS CULTURE

Enter a gift shop today and you are likely to find a whole universe of unicorns. They appear on calendars, address books, wrapping paper, playing cards, T-shirts, stained glass windows, book plates, canvas tote bags, key rings, jigsaw puzzles, jewelry, candles, stationery, kites, cocktail glasses, ice buckets, pillows. Unicorn night lights, lamps, and stuffed animals gaze out at us from shop windows. Nor are images of the unicorn reserved only for such items; open a phone book and you will probably see at least one business listed under U for unicorn—perhaps an employment agency, a record label, a film company, or a bookstore. They are pictured on the covers of paperback books and in the pages of mail-order catalogues. They have inspired films, songs, and poetry. Until very recently we saw the unicorn mainly in art museums. Today it has re-entered popular culture.

Its ubiquitous presence is somewhat of a surprise, for while the unicorn has its roots in several ancient cultures it is quintessentially a medieval

Ladies and Unicorns
by Gustave Moreau (1826–1896).

ABOVE AND OPPOSITE
Touch *from the* Lady and the
Unicorn *series. The sensuous nature
of the unicorn myth is clearly
expressed in these tapestries, five of
which represent the senses.*

animal. To the Greeks the unicorn was a little-known creature of some zoological interest. It was not sufficiently important to appear either in their mythology or in their art. But to the men and women of the Middle Ages and the Renaissance, the unicorn was more than just an animal. At no time was this more true than during the fifteenth century. Prior to that there had been for several centuries a brisk trade in unicorn horns, for the therapeutic (and aphrodisiac) properties of the horn were well known. People were acquainted too with the Biblical unicorn and the unicorn of Physiologus. They knew how a unicorn might be captured, and they knew what the virgin-capture story signified in Christianity.

It was in the fifteenth century, even as some people were beginning to doubt the unicorn's physical existence, that interest in the unicorn as a symbolic beast blossomed. Suddenly the artwork of the time was filled with unicorns. The unicorn was used to illustrate psalters, altars, and books of hours. It was carved into doorways, church pews, and wooden chests. Most notably it was woven into tapestries, including two famous sets, both made at the end of the fifteenth century: *The Hunt of the Unicorn*, now at The Cloisters in New York, and *The Lady and the Unicorn*, at the Cluny Museum in Paris. As the abundance of these artworks indicates, the unicorn had a special appeal to the Gothic imagination. Part of its attraction was that, by then, the unicorn had accrued an enormous amount of symbolism. It was a figure of profound meaning, of constant reverberations, implications, overtones. Possessing both strength and beauty, it referred to the spiritual world and to the world of the senses, and as a result it inspired great artwork.

The sensuous appeal of the unicorn is most clearly manifested in *The Lady and the Unicorn* tapestries. That well-loved set comprises six tapestries, five of which represent the senses. In the tapestry representing sight, the unicorn's legs are resting on the woman's lap and it is looking at itself in a mirror she is holding. In the tapestry representing touch, her hand is on its horn. As the ancient story indicates, a mutual attraction flows between the woman and the unicorn; the sexual aspect has always been implicit.

Even the depiction of the unicorn was sometimes seen as powerful in itself. In Germany an altar illustrating the hunt of the unicorn was believed to

have the miraculous ability to heal. Up to forty-four thousand pilgrims visited the shrine annually—a steady parade of the handicapped, the halt, and the helpless.

But times changed. In the fifteenth century the unicorn fulfilled an imaginative need that was largely symbolic. In the sixteenth century voyages of discovery across uncharted oceans permanently enlarged our concept of the world, while in Europe—where many thousands of women and girls were killed as witches—violence in the name of religion was common. At the Council of Trent in 1563, which confirmed many of the traditional beliefs of the Catholic Church against the challenges of the Protestant reformers, it was decreed that all

The Lion and the Unicorn
were fighting for the Crown;
The Lion Beat the Unicorn
all round about the town.

Some gave them white bread,
and some gave them brown;
Some gave them plum-cake,
and sent them out of town.

"unusual portrayals" of Christ in artwork were to be avoided unless given specific approval by the bishops. After this the unicorn was used much less frequently, and by the seventeenth, eighteenth and nineteenth centuries its mass appeal for the most part was gone. Only rarely did the unicorn appear in art and literature, although heraldic images persisted, most notably in the British Royal Arms. Not surprisingly, then, considering the heraldic coupling of the lion and the unicorn, the story that remained most vividly in public awareness was the old tale in which the lion captures the unicorn by chasing it until it sticks its horn into a tree and cannot escape. Edmund Spenser, in *The Faerie Queene*, tells the ancient story:

Like as a Lyon, whose imperiall powre
A prowd rebellious Vnicorne defies,
T'auoide the rash assault and wrathfull stowre
Of his fiers foe, him to a tree applies,
And when him running in full course he spies,
He slips aside; the whiles that furious beast
His precious horne, sought of his enimies,
Strikes in the stocke, ne thence can be releast,
But to the mighty victour yields a bounteous feast.

Illustrations from Ring o' Roses *by L. Leslie Brooke, 1922.*

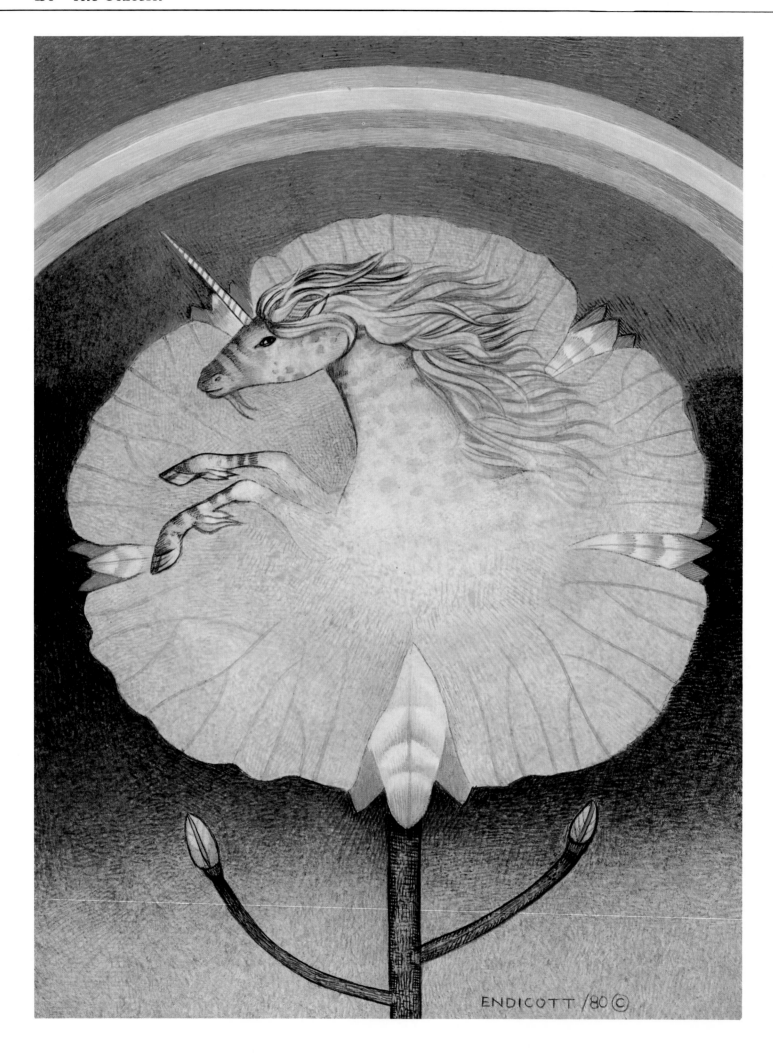

ENDICOTT /80 ©

Shakespeare refers to the same legend in "The Rape of Lucrece" and in *Julius Caesar*, when Decius Brutus remarks that Caesar "loves to hear that unicorns may be betrayed with trees."

It was not just in England, where the coat of arms was supported by the unicorn and the lion, that this story was remembered. In Germany, where the unicorn had been particularly loved, the story was also known. The Brothers Grimm, whose folk tales were first published in 1819, told of the Brave Little Tailor, who ventured into the forest to capture the unicorn and thus win the daughter of the king:

In a short while the unicorn came along and rushed at the tailor, meaning to run him straight through with his horn. "Not so fast!" said the tailor. "It's not as easy as all that." He stood still, waited until the unicorn was quite near him, and then jumped nimbly behind a tree. The unicorn charged full force and rammed into the tree. His horn went in and stuck so fast that he hadn't the strength to pull it out. He was caught. "I've got him," said the tailor. He came out from behind the tree, put the rope around the unicorn's neck, and, taking his ax, chopped the wood away from the horn. When this was done, he led the beast to the king.

Later in the nineteenth century Lewis Carroll, in *Through the Looking Glass*, also showed familiarity with the unicorn, but he portrayed the animal in an unexpected way:

At this moment, the Unicorn sauntered by them with his hands in his pockets . . . when his eye happened to fall upon Alice: he turned round instantly, and stood for some time looking at her with an air of the deepest disgust.
"What—is—this?" he said at last.
"This is a child!" Haigha replied eagerly, coming in front of Alice to introduce her. . . . "We only found it today. It's as large as life and twice as natural!"
"I always thought they were fabulous monsters!" said the Unicorn. "Is it alive?"
"It can talk," said Haigha solemnly.
The Unicorn looked dreamily at Alice, and said "Talk, child."
Alice could not help her lips curling up into a smile as she began: "Do you know, I always thought Unicorns were fabulous monsters, too? I never saw one alive before!"
"Well, now we *have* seen each other," said the Unicorn, "if you'll believe in me, I'll believe in you. Is that a bargain?"

OPPOSITE
". . . and from the heart of the blossom there appeared a unicorn. . ." *by James Endicott.*

BELOW
The Baby Unicorn, *contemporary bronze sculpture by Michael von Meyer.*

By this time, however, like other legends that once were strong, the unicorn had been relegated to the world of fantasy, of stories for children. Its former power was almost completely eroded, and by the beginning of the twentieth century the unicorn legend retained only a dim reflection of its former light. But it did not fade away completely.

Painting by Jacquelyn Sage from In Pursuit of the Unicorn, *Pomegranate Artbooks.*

Legends and myths, which arise to explain the world and to make something ordered out of it, are born and grow under certain cultural circumstances. When these circumstances change in some major way the beliefs which they engendered may also shift. Some of the images that contained those beliefs fade away entirely, such as the story of Prester John. Other images, which are stronger and have continued meaning, survive, although often in an attenuated fashion. Thus it is that while no one worships the Greek or Roman gods anymore, a number of their images—Venus, Cupid, Medusa, Mercury with his winged heels—still speak to us. But while the forms of these images still exist much of their content has disappeared and they have lost the essential character of their meaning. This process happens with many elements of culture, including folk tales, superstitions, elements of religion. Fairy tales, because they can seem threatening, have been stripped of some of their psychological integrity and force by popularizers of mass culture. The original Cinderella, for example, is a far stronger figure than Walt Disney makes her out to be, and the story itself is full of vengeance. In the Grimm tale, the stepsisters, who want to fit into Cinderella's tiny slipper, mutilate their feet by cutting off toes and heels; later, on Cinderella's wedding day, birds pluck out their eyes. These psychologically valid elements have been somewhat lost today, but the story still possesses enough resonance to be of perennial interest. Other images that were strong in the past have also been devitalized. The powerful, positive figures of the Amazon, that strong woman warrior who lives without men, and the witch, who can heal the body and control the forces of nature, have been distorted and trivialized, although recently the Women's Movement has reclaimed them. As weak as some stories and images become they survive because they still address themselves to some human need. This need gives them the potential to be regenerated.

In the twentieth century the unicorn, after centuries of obsolescence, has emerged in an unexpected guise. Its re-emergence was partially inspired by nineteenth-century investigations into mythology—including such peculiar and wonderful books as *The Unicorn: A Mythological Investigation* by Robert Brown, which approached the unicorn in terms of solar symbolism, a popular nineteenth-century concept later much ridiculed. In the beginning of this century, the unicorn began to appear as a symbol of strength. William Butler Yeats, who was fascinated by symbols of all kinds, published a play in 1908 called *The Unicorn from the Stars*. In it the one-horned beast becomes once more a complex and paradoxical symbol:

Martin: There were horses . . . white horses rushing by, with white shining riders . . . there was a horse without a rider, and someone caught me up and put me upon him, and we rode away, with the wind, like the wind. . . . Then I saw the horses we were on had changed to unicorns, and they began trampling the grapes and breaking them. . . . They tore down the wheat and trampled it on the stones, and then they tore down what was left of the grapes and crushed and bruised and trampled them. I smelt the wine, it was flowing on every side . . . everything was silent. . . . I saw a bright many-changing figure . . . it was holding up a shining vessel . . . (holds up arms) then the vessel

Detail from
Sanctuary *by Kirwan.*

fell and was broken with a great crash . . . then I saw the unicorns trampling it. They were breaking the world to pieces . . . when I saw the cracks coming, I shouted for joy! And I heard the command, "Destroy, destroy; destruction is the life-giver; destroy." . . . I am to destroy; destruction was the word the messenger spoke.
Father John: To destroy?
Martin: To bring again the old disturbed exalted life, the old splendour.

Unicorns *by Arthur B. Davies*
(1862–1928).

The unicorn here is once again a symbol of trans-formation, for this unicorn seeks a better world—or a return to a better world—through the purifying, purgative powers of destruction. Its purpose, like that of the Hindu god Siva, is to tear down and to renew. And if the play is a little heavy-handed at times, the unicorn is still elemental and untamed.

Other writers, including W. H. Auden, James Thurber, García Lorca, and Rainer Maria Rilke, were also drawn to this ferocious animal. Dylan Thomas, in his poem "And death shall have no dominion," refers to "unicorn evils," while William Carlos Williams, whose unicorn in *Paterson* is more benevolent, also pictures it in a powerful way:

The Unicorn
             the white one-horned beast
                          thrashes about
root toot a toot!
             faceless among the stars
                          calling
for its own murder

This unicorn is a sacrificial one, analagous to the medieval animal that was drawn to the virgin. It is concerned with death, destruction, and, simultaneously, creation—a linkage made more explicit later on:

             The Unicorn
has no match
             or mate   •   the artist
             has no peer •
Death
has no peer

The creative powers of the artist and the destructive powers of death are cut from the same cloth as the powers of the unicorn—that is, they are transforming. This unicorn is spiritual not in the fuzzy, kindhearted way we think of today, but in the strong, direct way that characterizes true metamorphosis.

Gradually the creature with one horn was being reborn. But it had not yet reached a mass audience. Two events changed that. In the mid-1930s, John D. Rockefeller, Jr., made a gift to The Cloisters of the set of tapestries known as *The Hunt of the Unicorn*. Woven around 1500, probably in Brussels, as a wedding gift, the set of seven tapestries was owned for several centuries by the La Rochefoucauld family in France. In 1680 the tapestries hung

Detail from
The Unicorn Leaps the Stream.

OPPOSITE
The Start of the Hunt,
a late fifteenth-century tapestry
from The Hunt of the Unicorn.

in their Parisian town house, and by 1728 they were in the Château of Verteuil. There they remained until the French Revolution, when peasants from the village ransacked the castle. From 1793 until the middle of the next century, the tapestries were used to cover fruit trees and vegetables to keep them from freezing. Then the La Rochefoucaulds discovered them in a barn and the tapestries were once again installed in the Château. When they were exhibited in New York in 1922 Rockefeller saw them for the first time. A year later they were his, wall decorations for his private residence. Five years later, however, they were on exhibition at the Metropolitan Museum of Art, and later Rockefeller donated them to The Cloisters, where they were hanging in May 1938 when that facility first opened. Shortly after the beginning of World War II they were removed for safe-keeping, but in 1944 they were hung once more. The tapestries, immediately popular, provided the ultimate visual image of the unicorn: a graceful, horse-like animal, creamy white, with a long spiraling horn, cloven hoofs, a curled beard, and a delicately plumed tail. It is this picture, present as well in *The Lady and the Unicorn* series, which even now defines the unicorn.

In 1945 another event occurred which helped to solidify the unicorn's position in modern consciousness. Tennessee Williams' highly successful play, *The Glass Menagerie,* opened on Broadway. In one scene Laura Wingfield, a shy, lonely, and slightly crippled young woman, meets for the first time in six years a boy she had admired in high school. She shows him her collection of glass animals, and in particular she lets him hold her favorite:

Jim: What kind of a thing is this one supposed to be?
Laura: Haven't you noticed the single horn on its
   forehead?
Jim: A unicorn, huh?
Laura: Mmmm-hmmm!
Jim: Unicorns, aren't they extinct in the modern
   world?
Laura: I know!
Jim: Poor little fellow, he must feel sort of lonesome.

They dance, and during the waltz her prize possession is swept to the floor and its horn broken off. As the young man—the "gentleman caller"— takes his leave, after telling Laura and her mother

*Unicorn sculptures
in sterling silver with opal eyes
by Christalene Loren.*

The unicorn is known in Japan as the kirin. Featured here on the label for Kirin Beer, by far the most popular beer in Japan, the kirin was said to have appeared to the mother of Confucius before his birth. The Kirin Beer label has remained virtually the same since it was first introduced in 1889.

that he is engaged to be married, Laura gives him as a souvenir the broken unicorn.

This image, while clearly based upon the old connection between the unicorn and the virgin, helped to provide a new and immensely popular image of the unicorn. In the play, as in other instances where it is used, the unicorn is a symbol with sexual and physical connotations. Like Laura, the unicorn in *The Glass Menagerie* is fragile, vulnerable, pathetic, alone.

The last tapestry in *The Hunt of the Unicorn* also has a sense of this aloneness, although the unicorn there displays potential strength. This unicorn, which appears to be bleeding although in fact it is only stained with the juice of the pomegranates above it, is chained to the tree and walled in with a low fence. Clearly it could leap the fence if it so chose; but it does not, and the image as a result is one of self-imposed loneliness, even though this tapestry is often interpreted as symbolizing the captured lover. As the virgin-capture story implies, the unicorn is a figure simultaneously of sexuality

"These continued rumors that I don't exist are making it very difficult for me to obtain credit!"

Unicorn
by Laurie Noble.

and sublimation. The unicorn in the tapestry is both bereft of love and a prisoner of love, its erotic quality denied by its isolation. It is chained, restrained, solitary.

It is this particular unicorn—the unicorn in captivity—that has proved so immensely popular. It has been reproduced, sometimes well and often poorly, on scores of objects. Probably more than any other picture, it epitomizes our contemporary vision of the unicorn.

As an image of isolation, loneliness, and alienation, this unicorn has a distinctly twentieth-century cast to it. Loved especially by women, its appeal is to those who feel powerless—and its appeal is tremendous. If it has lost its freedom, so have we—a concept dealt with explicitly in Audre Lorde's poem, "The Black Unicorn." We too feel chained, fenced in, isolated. But if we sense a pang when we look at the unicorn in the tapestry, our feeling is not a hopeless one. The alertness of the unicorn's body and the directness of its gaze tell

ABOVE
A James Thurber drawing illustrating his story "The Unicorn in the Garden."

California orange crate label, ca. 1925.

Stonehenge I *by Jonathan Meader from* In Pursuit of the Unicorn.

Pigicorn in Captivity *by June Sobel.*

us that this unicorn still possesses intrinsic power.

In many recent portrayals, however, the unicorn has been made bland and weak. It is often seen as a pretty animal—alone in a wooded glen, bedecked with flowers, surrounded by butterflies and rainbows. This creature has been made nice. Its fierceness has been lost, along with its imprisoning collar and chain. In the Middle Ages, the unicorn was a sacrificial symbol; by its death, it improved the human situation. (The idea that an animal sacrifice could accomplish this goes back to ancient times, but it is represented even in Christianity by the equation of Christ with the lamb—the traditional sacrificial animal—and with the unicorn.) In the medieval stories—the virgin-capture and the unicorn and the lion—the unicorn dies. But today's unicorn no longer has the power it once had, and the implications of death and transformation are for the most part expunged (although the connection with death still exists in such popular novels as Phyllis Whitney's *The Golden Unicorn* and Jay Halpern's *The Jade Unicorn*). Today the unicorn has become a wish, a dream. In commercial art it is sometimes as weak and charming as a new-born colt; it is pictured in an idyllic landscape and it is thoroughly tame. It appears not primarily in the way that Yeats or William Carlos Williams saw it, but instead, as in *The Glass Menagerie*, as an emblem of escape. As such, it is often used in science fiction and in fantasy.

Sometimes, the unicorn figures in the title of such books. It acts as a totem, an indication of the unique and the exotic, and occasionally as a reference—to another, better time, or to the actual legends of the unicorn. Roger Zelazny's *Sign of the Unicorn*, Fletcher Pratt's *The Well of the Unicorn*, and Andre Norton's *Year of the Unicorn* are all books of this sort. In Anne McCaffrey's short-story collection *Get Off the Unicorn* the fabulous one-horned beast appears only in the title, although dragons play a part within the text. In other books the unicorn appears anthropomorphically. In C.S. Lewis's *The Last Battle* (seventh in the *Chronicles of Narnia* series) a unicorn named Jewel accompanies the other characters in a loyal but bumbling way. Madeleine L'Engle's fantasy for children, *A Swiftly Tilting Planet*, features Gaudior, an active, strong, unicorn, winged like Pegasus (a concept that also appears in popular art), who is able to help the human, a young boy, and to influence the course of history. The most well-known unicorn is Peter S. Beagle's *The Last Unicorn* (which has been made into an animated film). This unicorn actively seeks others of her kind in a world populated by flawed humans and imaginary beings. The time is the mythical past. The place is a magical land. The unicorn's purpose is to find community, to free her fellow unicorns, to destroy evil, and to restore life and power and meaning. Her search is a difficult and dangerous one but it is precisely this struggle that summarizes our feelings about unicorns.

Not since the fifteenth century has the unicorn had such an enormous appeal. It is easy to see why. In a world suffering from pollution, the unicorn

can purify water with a single dip of its horn. In a world where animals are becoming extinct, the unicorn can never die. In a world where we might literally blow ourselves up at any moment, the unicorn harkens back to another time and a better life. The unicorn symbolizes sensitivity coupled with strength, the lure of sexuality and nature linked with the power of purity and truth. Today, when it is difficult to believe in these things any longer, the unicorn reminds us of a time when good existed—when unicorns existed. In a time when the future is looking bleak, the unicorn is a symbol not just of hope but of strength; it tells us that the unattainable is worth striving for, worth searching for, worth believing in—even if it exists only in our minds.

Nineteenth-century scrimshaw pie crimper made of whale ivory.

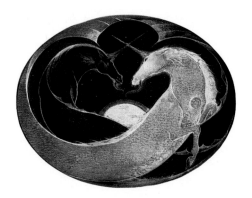

XII
THE CELESTIAL UNICORN

Rains crept slowly over the world and people were glad that the drought was over. For the first time, there was no famine; the world was blanketed with green. But the rains continued, more insistently than before, and the land became too wet. The traditional crops could no longer be grown; mushrooms and ferns sprouted in the fields, and slabs of bracket fungus formed white shelves along the trunks of fruit trees, while further south, winding tendrils and fleshy flowers grew everywhere. And the rains kept coming.

Then, gradually, it turned cold. In some places snow fell for the first time, and everyone watched as shapes they had known for a lifetime were obliterated by the chill swirling powder. Farmers standing on their flooded plots of land and old desert nomads, shivering as snow sifted over the sand dunes, were the first to feel the fear. And it kept growing colder. The white rays of the sun at noon seemed dimmer than before, and the sky was pale. Winter was more severe than anyone could remember, and when the calendar indicated it was

"After a while the unicorn began to feel fatigued and isolated, even though it had always been a solitary being."
Painting by Susan Boulet.

time for a thaw, nothing changed. After several years had passed, everyone understood that winter was now eternal.

Tropical jungle trees that had once harbored monkeys and parrots were now covered with ice, frozen in rocky splendor. Hardier northern plants—the fir, the pine and the birch—survived for a while, but the temperatures dropped day by day. Many of the northern trees froze and cracked in the wind and the scruffy plants of the tundra spread south and were soon the only form of vegetation anywhere.

By that time most of the animals had died too, and their frozen carcasses littered the land. The tropical animals perished quickly. Other animals grew thicker coats and endured for a while, but eventually only the animals already adapted to the frigid temperatures lived: the polar bear, the leopard seal, the reindeer, the skua with its enormous wings. The unicorn, like many other animals, had little difficulty at first in adjusting to the cold. It grew a heavier coat, which provided protection from the numbing air and the snow that stung. For months it wandered through the pale translucence of this unexpected and empty world. After a while the unicorn began to feel fatigued and isolated, even though it had always been a solitary being. Its search for shelter, for a tree to sleep under, seemed futile, and it grew weak and afraid. One day, when the sun set very early and the wind blew sharp and steadily, it collapsed beneath a blue-white drift of snow shaped like a wave. Snuggling

into the curl of the wave, the unicorn lay down with its head upon its hoofs. It fell asleep almost immediately, and as the wind blew, the wave crested over until the unicorn was completely covered, just a bulge in the endless pale landscape. Beneath the snow the unicorn slept unaware, and gradually its body froze. Snow continued to swell and billow; diamonds of ice spun in the wind; and slowly the air turned to frozen crystal. But the unicorn did not die. . . .

Like the plants and the animals, most of the people perished. At first, in areas that once had been warm year-round they trembled and froze for lack of adequate heat and shelter. Others, numbly gathered in increasingly smaller groups, carefully rationed food saved in warmer times. But there came a day when that too was gone, and after a while few of those people remained. Eventually, only the hardy and the resourceful survived. Banded together in small groups, they learned to wrest food and shelter from the icy world where they now found themselves, and they began to build new settlements. Babies were born who had never known another climate, and they grew up and had children themselves. And this world of cold began to seem right and proper—the way it had always been, would always be.

In one community a few cabins covered with skins huddled together on a high, raw prairie. Reindeer wandered through the village, while in the distance mountains loomed, white and blue with shadow. A few old people still lived here who

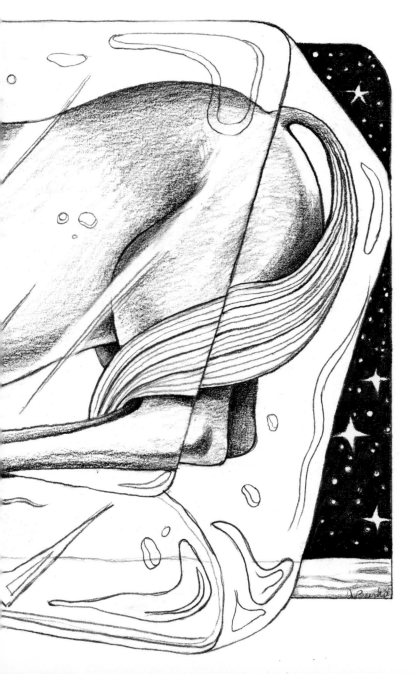

"The ice was still there, becoming clearer as it melted, and she could see the unicorn inside. Its horn glistened like an icicle."
Pencil drawing by Dianne Burke.

recalled the way the world had been when they were children, and it was one of their few pleasures to tell their memories to the younger people of the settlement, many of whom were distinctly uninterested. But one little girl, named Xana, loved to hear her grandparents' tales. She would sit quietly on a rug in their cabin and listen carefully. The cabin was small and dark, for animal skins, nailed to the walls to keep out the cold, also blocked most of the light. But through the occasional gaps and tears in the skins came spots of light—sunfruit— which quivered on the floor. The old people, wrapped in their thick furs, watched these spots slowly slide across the floor, and they would talk about the world when it was warm. Although they enjoyed the familiar litany they no longer really listened to each other, and so while one spoke, the others nodded and dreamed. Only Xana listened, fascinated by this picture of a different world.

Her grandfather, whose father had been a farmer, described how the land had once been covered, not with snow and frost, but with green plants. He told about the grasses, the prickly hedges of roses and holly, the sprawling squash vines, and the yearly cycle of the trees. Now there was nothing, he said, and his face had a sour look to it. He would try to fathom why the great change had come, and he always came back to the same explanation. It was, he said, a just punishment from the gods, but he did not know for what.

Her grandmother began to talk then, and she spoke, as she often did, about the animals. There were so many! she said, and all so different. Xana looked then at the border of the rug, which was woven with the shapes of animals. Her grandmother had told her about many of them—the horse, the enormous elephant, the hateful snake, the lion. The one that Xana liked the best was woven into the corner of the rug, a graying white against the deep blue. It looked a little like a horse, she thought, except that a delicate horn sprouted from its head and its tail was like a lion's. Once her grandmother had told her that it was called a unicorn, but that she had never seen one. Now as her grandmother talked, Xana stared at the design of the animal and she moved her hand back and forth across the weave. In one direction it felt rough, and in the other smooth, and she wondered which way

the real creature would be. The two most interesting parts of the unicorn were the horn and the eye. She touched the tip of the horn with her finger, and then she touched the eye. The eye was only a speck on the carpet, just a tiny dot, but sometimes in certain light it seemed to glimmer. She leaned down to look at it more closely, and when she was almost touching it with her own eye she could see the tiny fibers. Little bits of light were caught in the twisted threads. She focused on one spot of light, and as she looked at it, it seemed to her that it grew slightly larger and she could see what the real unicorn must look like. It was pale, unmoving, with its head resting upon its hoofs, and, although it seemed so far away, she could feel its cool presence with some distant part of herself. For a long time she gazed at its long, snow-colored face, its silvery lashes and lucent horn, all entrapped in ice. The creature was the most beautiful thing she had ever seen, she thought, and she longed to be with it. She felt a warmth spread through her forehead. And then the unicorn opened its violet eyes.

For a long time she stared at it, until someone called her name. It was her grandfather. She looked up at him quizzically. He and her grandmother and another old man were laughing at her. She smiled weakly, and they returned to their conversation. Once more she bent down to the unicorn, but this time, when she stared at the eye nothing happened, and it remained a figure woven into the corner of a rug.

In the days that followed Xana often got down on her knees and stared at the design. Sometimes nothing happened, but at other times she felt her forehead glow and it was as though she could see through the rough weave into the shining eyes of the real unicorn. She could sense its cold and its confinement, and she longed to see it free. But as soon as she looked elsewhere, or sometimes even when she blinked, the thin thread of connection between her and the unicorn was broken, and she could not always recapture it. She wondered where the creature was, and then one day, while she was watching the fire, she thought she knew. It was at the foot of the mountains—and she was sure she could find it.

The next morning she pulled on her heavy leggings, stuck some food inside her jacket, and when no one was looking, slipped out through the door.

She started to walk toward the jagged white peaks on the horizon. She thought it was probably a long way but that if she started out early enough she could reach the unicorn before nightfall. But before she had even passed the outskirts of the settlement a neighbor came running after her, picked her up, and brought her home. Again and again she tried to go to the mountains and the thick block of ice she knew was there, but someone always stopped her. Finally, determined, she forced herself to stay up at night, and while everyone slept, she sneaked out through the door, past the clutter of cabins and then across the snow-covered plains to the mountains. She trudged slowly over the crusted snow and she watched the moon climb across the sky, and still she was not at the mountain. By the time the sun came up she was very tired, and yet she had not reached even the foothills. She was tempted to lie down and take a short nap, something she had always been warned against, when she heard distant shouts. She turned around. A sled was coming toward her; inside were her father, her grandfather, and several men of the village. As soon as the sled was close enough, her father yanked the reins and the reindeer came to a halt. He jumped out, picked her up, and shook her. "Where are you going?" he asked, and she tried to tell him about the animal in the block of ice at the foot of the mountain. But he barely listened to her, and she was swept into the sled and back to the settlement.

Several nights later she set out once again. This time she made a special effort to run as much as possible in order to reach the mountains more quickly. Once she fell, and snow slipped into her mittens and down her jacket. She shook them out, shivered, and kept running. In the morning the sled overtook her once again. Her father and the other men were angry at her, but this time her grandfather spoke up and insisted that they hear her tale. The others listened, smirking, to Xana's description of the unicorn trapped in a block of ice. She pointed toward the mountains. "It's there," she said. No one wanted to pay much credence to her story, but her grandfather, who had been watching her gravely, demanded that they take her to the mountain. The others did not want to do this, but because he was old and venerated they

"More than anything else Xana wanted to be with the unicorn." Painting by Susan Boulet.

gave in. Xana climbed into the sled, and the reindeer trotted ahead toward the mountain.

When they reached the foothills it was midmorning. Xana was sleepy, but whenever she shut her eyes the vision of the unicorn swam before her. Its eyes were open, its pupils dilated. She knew exactly where it was now, and she directed the men.

At last they arrived. She jumped out of the sled and ran to what looked like a large, snow-covered rock. She began to push the soft snow away. Underneath was ice, cracked and white—and in it she could see, just vaguely, the outline of the unicorn. At first the men saw nothing, but then one of them thought that maybe he too could see an animal. And although they felt foolish, they began to survey the giant block. They walked around and around, taking measurements with their hands. Finally, as the reindeer pawed at the moss hidden beneath the snow, the men took out their picks and axes. They hacked at the block, chipped at it with their tools until they were covered with icy splinters, and pulled it with their ropes until at last a large chunk containing a dim shape fell slightly forward from the mass of ice. After they tied it with leather thongs to the back of the sled the men harnessed the reindeer, and they all piled in. The return trip was slow, for the reindeer were tired and the load was heavy.

In the village Xana fell asleep at once. When she awoke her journey seemed like a dream. She sat by the hearth stone and watched the fire. She was mesmerized by the flames, by the tiny jumping beings with uplifted arms and pointed heads who told their sad and hysterical stories. When the heat became too much, when she felt her skin pull tight, she moved away from the fire, opened the door and went outside. The ice was still there, becoming clearer as it melted, and she could see the unicorn inside. Its horn glistened like an icicle; its head was still upon its hoofs; but the tufted tail had started to flicker, and the sides of the unicorn heaved.

The next day a celebration was held. All the villagers wore white fox fur, and there was music—although the singers, swaying slightly back and forth, changed pitch hardly at all, and the song was as unvaried as the landscape. A torch was

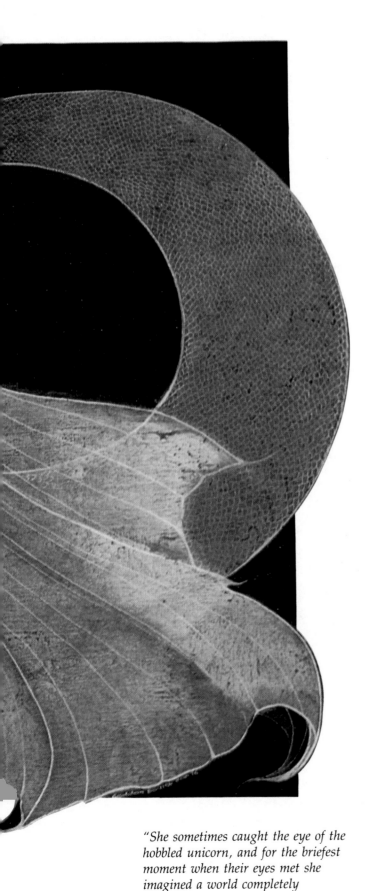

"She sometimes caught the eye of the hobbled unicorn, and for the briefest moment when their eyes met she imagined a world completely different, filled with warmth and color."
Painting by Susan Boulet.

passed in a wide circle around the block of ice; slowly it melted and the unicorn started to emerge. The people were astounded. At first no one dared touch the unicorn. But finally one of the elders approached while it still struggled for breath and gingerly placed his hands on the unicorn's thin flanks. As it thawed the unicorn shivered and tried to stand. When it finally succeeded the same man who had patted it tied leather hobbles about its wobbling legs and brought it food: seal meat and fish heads, which it refused to eat, and a few shavings from a scruffy bush. Daily the villagers came

"When it was not serving as a beast of burden, the unicorn was tied to the heavy boulders and its feet were hobbled with bands of leather." Pencil drawing by Dianne Burke.

to feed the unicorn and to pay it homage, for clearly it was an extraordinary creature and its appearance, they thought, must herald something wonderful. Throughout the summer they watched the unicorn, which was docile and weak at first but grew increasingly skittish. The hobbles were tightened, and the unicorn was put in a harness and tied to heavy boulders. The people in the tiny settlement looked every day upon the unicorn, and they wondered.

Gradually the wonder wore away and was replaced with acceptance. The elders, who had been so worshipful, saw that nothing had changed in the village, and they came up with a new plan. When it was time to go in search of whale they harnessed the unicorn to the cargo sled. The chief hunter of the village sat in the back of the sled as the unicorn pulled the bulky vehicle. Its endurance, they found, was greater than that of the reindeer who normally pulled their sleds, and unlike that animal, the unicorn did not relentlessly follow the moss. It became a tradition, then; every year at whale season the unicorn was tied to the sled and, all alone, hauled the heavy carcass back to the village.

When it was not serving as a beast of burden, the unicorn was tied to the heavy boulders and its feet were hobbled with bands of leather. During these first few years Xana often wandered out of the hut during daylight hours and sat near the unicorn. Its sadness seemed so great that once she put her arms around the unicorn's neck and hugged it. To her surprise the unicorn breathed an enormous sigh, and the frozen puffs of its breath opened like flowers.

In summer Xana sat outside and watched her mother stitch skins together with a three-sided ivory needle. In winter she stayed in the cabin as her mother heated fat and melted handfuls of snow in a heavy pot to which she added marrow and blood until it formed a viscous syrup. Its smell permeated the air, and Xana hated it. But she had been forbidden to play outside on winter days, for she invariably wandered away from the cabin and toward the unicorn. One time, her parents spent many hours looking for her and finally found her asleep in a pale blue mound of snow behind the great boulders that now fenced in the creature. More than anything else Xana wanted to be with the unicorn, but the villagers, who feared it, did not allow her to do that. Her winter days were gloomy ones.

Year by year, as Xana grew, she found more reasons to leave the cabin, and her parents worried. She wanted to go hunting but was not allowed to, and when the children learned the reindeer game, she always was the one to run and hold the horns upon her head. When she did this she sometimes caught the eye of the hobbled unicorn, and for the briefest moment when their eyes met she imagined a world completely different, filled with warmth and color. And then she felt the rope descend about her branched horns, and the game was over.

The unicorn was trained to do other tasks: to crack holes in the ice with its horn for fishing, to locate cloudberries, and, most of all, to haul. As its tasks increased the unicorn grew more disconsolate. Everywhere it looked it saw a sea of cold: ice and stones, snow and sky. The unicorn dimly remembered another world, and how that world had died, a soft surcease in whirling clouds of snow. That life existed no longer, and so the unicorn continued to pull the heavy carcasses of bear and seal and whale.

Soon Xana was too old to play the reindeer game, and she put down the horns forever. Her parents betrothed her to a young man known for his skill at carving and for his perpetual silence. They were married in a ceremony at midsummer. The villagers sang their song for the young couple, and at the end of the ceremony, when Xana and her new husband were carting away their gifts in a painted sled, they stopped briefly before the unicorn. The unicorn whinnied. No one had heard it do that before; everyone took it for an omen, and their predictions for the young couple were unhappy ones.

When, after a few years, Xana failed to bear children, everyone felt the predictions had been fulfilled, for the marriage was a failure. At night Xana sometimes wandered outside, watching the unicorn through the pile of boulders that now imprisoned it. The council had appointed a guard to watch over the unicorn, and the man to whom they originally gave that task was now growing old and listless; yet every night, when it was dark, he checked the leather straps, put a bucket of melted snow by the unicorn, and made certain that all the heavy boulders were in place. He sat there all night. Occasionally he would peek in through the chinks in the stone wall, but the unicorn always turned away from him.

When Xana looked at the unicorn it always gazed back at her, and a quiet understanding passed between them. Yet sometimes it frightened her, for when she looked at its sad face for too long a time, the smoky clouds of its breath in the cold air began to take on new shapes; a sphere of breath might turn into a twisted column of birds, or a swaying field of snowgrass, or a tangle of stars. She could not move away; its violet eyes held her, and more than once the guard had to shake her by the shoulders to get her attention and tell her to go home.

And so it was that the villagers began to avoid Xana. Some had seen her at the unicorn's rock fence, her dark hair bound tightly but uncovered and dotted with snowflakes; others could not forget the unicorn's strange whinny at her wedding years before. Xana spent little time with the other villagers. She did her chores without complaint, addressed few words to her husband, and mourned the narrow circumference of her life—boiled bones, low fires, carcasses stripped pink. She suspected there might be something wrong with her, imagined that she had been inhabited by the spirit of someone long dead. She confided her fear to her husband and as a result was visited in her cabin by the elders who sang their ritual song for seven days and at the end of that time burned most of her skins so that she had to spend months stretching and sewing new ones. From then on she was silent about her worries, but nevertheless they plagued her.

Xana grew older. The years passed, but the unicorn was unchanged. Occasionally at night, although her body had grown stiff, she would pull on her heavy clothes and wander out into the center of the settlement to peer in at the unicorn. When the moon was new it would be almost too dark to see the creature, and she would have to look for a few seconds before she saw the shimmer of the horn; but when the moon was full the moonlight reflected from the snow illumined everything, and she could see each detail of the unicorn's face. There was longing in it, she thought, and infinite patience. And then the guard would shoo her away, and she would trudge sadly home.

One winter day Xana spent many hours skinning a walrus, a task she hated. She went to bed exhausted, her fingers cracked and numb, but sleep did not come. Finally, when it was almost morning, she pulled on her fur jackets and walked outside. The sky was clear, the recent snow still soft upon the ground. She walked to the center of the village, and even from a distance she could see the large rocks piled in a circle around the unicorn. When she reached them she walked especially quietly, for she always hoped for a few extra seconds to watch the unicorn before the guard made her return

home. She went to her usual place—a spot where the space between the stones was large enough to put her hand through, if she dared. The unicorn was staring at her. She still thought it the most beautiful thing she had ever seen, and she longed, as always, to see it leap and run. She watched it for a few moments—and heard nothing. Perhaps the guard did not know she was there. Slowly she pulled off her fur mitten and put her hand through the space between the rocks. The unicorn came closer. When she stretched her arm out it nuzzled her hand and her palm tingled. She stood there for longer than she had ever thought possible, and still the guard did not approach her. She withdrew her hand and walked to the entrance, where a single boulder in front of the opening kept the unicorn prisoner. The boulder was in place; the guard was fast asleep, resting against one of the other rocks. She had never thought such a thing could happen. She stepped over the guard's outstretched legs. He turned on his side and wheezed. She stopped, afraid he would wake up, but his breathing quickly returned to the quiet hills of sleep, and she pressed her body against the boulder in the doorway. It did not move; she pressed against it harder and felt it creak against the snow. Then she picked up the guard's staff, jammed it against the rock, and pried the heavy boulder away from the opening. She stepped inside.

Within the circle of stones the unicorn waited. Its tail flicked back and forth and its eyes were bright, but it made no sound. Xana approached it carefully, stretching out her hand once more to it. In its leather hobbles it stumbled toward her. She put her hands on the unicorn's sides and rubbed it several times. Its coat was smooth in one direction and rough in the other and its long mane shone silver. Suddenly she imagined riding the unicorn; the same thought seemed to come to the unicorn, who rubbed gently against her and knelt down. She carefully put one leg over the unicorn, righted herself upon its back, and held the warm neck. The unicorn stood and slowly stepped out of the stone prison. When they had gone a short distance the guard awoke. "Stop!" he yelled, and began calling to the other villagers. Xana nervously looked behind her—the guard was running after them and in his hands he held a length of rope that he was tying into a lasso. In a moment he would capture them. The unicorn's pace was so slow—almost limping, she thought—and then she remembered that the unicorn was still hobbled. She slid down off its back and untied the leather restraints. Behind her she heard the whoosh of the lasso, but the guard had not practiced with the rope for many years, and the lasso fell short. As she pulled herself back on the unicorn she heard the rope again as the guard whirled it in the air and prepared to whip it out toward them. Leaning forward, she whispered to the unicorn. "Run," she said. "Run fast as you can." The unicorn's ears perked up, and, just as it began to trot, she felt the rope nick her arm. "Run," she repeated, and she gripped the mane tightly.

The unicorn broke into a gallop. It kicked its heels into the air and the snow rose up in a mist around them. She could still hear the shouts of the guard and of some of the other villagers too. But they were far behind—and the unicorn still galloped.

The village faded behind them. They could hear only the whirring of wind and the drumming of hoofs on frozen tundra. Once they were beyond the frontier guards, she thought, nothing could stop them. They galloped through a wide white valley surrounded by mountains. With every step the unicorn took, Xana felt a wild exultation inside her and she started to laugh. She clung to the unicorn's mane; the unicorn's strength grew, and they went faster and faster through the valley of snow. The sun's oblique rays were lying across the white expanse, and here and there a few stunted trees cast long thin shadows across the snow. They galloped on. At the foot of the pass over the mountain the unicorn leaped forward. Full of anticipation, Xana took a deep breath; on the slopes above the pass were the guards, and after that—no one knew. The unicorn was sure-footed climbing the rocky incline. As they neared the top a shout broke the silence.

"Halt!" yelled a voice—and the sound echoed, bouncing against the surrounding peaks. Xana looked up and saw a small group of fur-clad guards on the boulder-strewn slope above them. The men called out again, and one of them took an ivory bugle from his belt and began to blow. The hollow, nasal sound reverberated in the air—and all along the slopes above them other guards appeared, some carrying clubs, others carrying ropes and long hunting knives. Xana's throat was dry and her

"Suddenly she imagined riding the unicorn."
Painting by Dianne Burke.

breath came quickly. The guards were shouting to each other, but she could not make out their words, and the unicorn continued on. The man who had blown the bugle disappeared momentarily behind a boulder. Xana heard a shout—and the boulder slowly broke away from its place on the mountain and began to tumble down. The unicorn sprinted. Another boulder began the bumpy descent, and another, and another. The boulders and the harsh cries of the guards loosened the hard-packed snow so that jagged crusts of snow rolled and tumbled down the slopes along with the heavy rocks. A crack, another rumble, and sharp-edged chunks of snow and stones came hurtling down and rolling clouds of snow pitched past them. Xana felt the icy needles as they pricked her face, and her legs were struck by tumbling rocks. A huge wave of snow swept toward them, taller than they and crashing fast, and Xana felt its wind rushing down. As the crest reached them the unicorn stumbled, then increased its speed again.

Xana pressed her face to its neck; the unicorn took a tremendous leap forward; and they were flying, slowly, while the snow churned under them; and all about the air was filled with stinging shards. Gently they rose through clouds of snow, and as the guards shouted and the avalanche boomed and crashed below, they soared higher and higher until Xana could see beyond the mountain tops and into the unknown land beyond. It was snow-covered, mountainous, bleak—and then it too grew distant and the guards faded away in the blue shadows of the mountains. With a jubilant cry she tossed her sealskin cap—she could see it tumbling back—and her long gray hair fanned out behind her. The unicorn kept bounding along as if on an invisible road, and the icy crystals in the air whirled by in pastel arcs. They rode the hyperborean wind through the blue sky, through the wet and puffy clouds, toward the sun, and when night came they flew into pulsing puddles of color that floated across the sky.

They ran past the moon and past Mars glowing red, the lightning of Jupiter, Saturn's airy rings; and then the stars were swimming past them, shining blue, yellow, white, red; and they felt themselves growing; they were larger and larger; their bodies were filled with space and they could touch everywhere at once. A comet, hurtling at them like a giant snowball, made Xana wince, but they passed through it as they had through the clouds, and afterward they rode upon its tail. Meteors occasionally darted past, and still they grew, and then they saw ahead of them the centaur Sagittarius, half man, half horse. Xana waved her arm at him, and they galloped on, past Ophiocus the physician, who wrestled with a snake and nodded familiarly to the unicorn, and past the scorpion who pulled away at the unicorn's approach. They soared over the scales of Libra and toward Virgo, the goddess of the harvest, who held out a tassel of wheat to them. The unicorn pranced and neighed when the virgin waved at them, and slowed down a bit, and yet they rode forward some more, and Xana's laughter rang across the Milky Way. They rode past the lion, past the crab, and then two dogs began to bark in greeting, a tiny one with a wagging tail and a great one, and Xana and the unicorn felt they were about to burst with happiness, for they had flown through half the Zodiac and could go wherever they chose, surrounded by creatures at enormous distances. The two dogs were so friendly that the unicorn bounded toward them, past Castor and Pollux, toward the hunter Orion who swept his arm across the heavens and welcomed them to stay. So they came to rest by the banks of the River Eridanus. The stars, pale prisms of fire, filled them with their light, and whenever the people of Xana's village look up on clear nights, they can see her there, an old woman on a unicorn, riding across the sky.

"The unicorn took a tremendous leap forward; and they were flying, slowly, while the snow churned under them." Painting by Dianne Burke.

Annotated Bibliography

Illustration from a fourteenth-century Persian manuscript.

Baring-Gould, Sabine. *Curious Myths of the Middle Ages.* London: Longmans, Green and Co., 1906. Reprinted in 1977 by Christian Classics, Westminster, Md.
Although it hardly mentions the unicorn, this book, originally published in 1866 by a prolific English writer, is a compendium of medieval beliefs. Among the topics discussed are Prester John, Bishop Hatto, and amazing coincidences having to do with numbers and days of the week.

Beagle, Peter S. *The Last Unicorn.* New York: The Viking Press, 1968. A fantasy novel, written with grace and humor, in which the last unicorn on earth, assisted by Schmendrick the Magician and Molly Grue, searches for the lost members of her kind and has a host of wonderful adventures.

Beer, Robert Rüdiger. *Unicorn: Myth and Reality.* Translated by Charles M. Stern. New York and London: Van Nostrand Reinhold Co., 1977.
An illustrated history that discusses all aspects of the unicorn—from its early appearances in the Bible and Physiologus to contemporary (primarily German) literature. One of the basics.

Bernheimer, Richard. *Wild Men in the Middle Ages: A Study in Art, Sentiment, and Demonology.* Cambridge, Massachusetts: Harvard University Press, 1952.
An exhaustive and interesting study, also illustrated, of one of the strangest medieval beliefs.

Borges, Jorge Luis, with Guerrero, Margarita. *The Book of Imaginary Beings.* Revised, enlarged, and translated by Norman Thomas di Giovanni. New York: E. P. Dutton and Co., 1969.
In the preface Borges writes, "As we all know, there is a kind of lazy pleasure in useless and out-of-the-way erudition." With 120 entries written in Borges' inimitable style, this book provides a great deal of that sort of pleasure. Sections on the unicorn are basic and short. Unlike other bestiaries this book, which discusses creatures of many cultures, also touches upon various literary monsters, including the creations of Kafka, Poe, and C. S. Lewis.

Brown, Robert. *The Unicorn: A Mythological Investigation.* London: Longmans, Green and Co., 1881.
This book is disappointing to anyone looking for an overall investigation of the topic. It can also be distressing to those especially fond of accepted sentence structure. But for people interested in solar mythology, whereby almost everything is interpreted as relating to the sun and the moon, and for those who understand the arcane language of heraldry, this weird, unique book is a delight. According to Odell Shepard, it is "a wild book, but, like all its author's productions, a brilliant one, full of recondite learning and startling surmises."

Clark, Anne. *Beasts and Bawdy: A Book of Fabulous and Fantastical Beasts.* New York: Taplinger Publishing Co., 1975.
Not a bestiary, this book includes basic background information as well as discussions about the sex lives and other peculiar behaviors of the beasts, both real and imaginary. It also examines various medicinal uses for which the medieval mind thought parts of these animals particularly useful. Illustrated.

Clébert, Jean-Paul. *Bestiare Fabuleux.* Paris: Editions Albin Michel, 1971.
This illustrated dictionary of animal symbolism considers the animals from the varied viewpoints of history, mythology, psychology, art, and the occult sciences. It includes symbolic analysis often unavailable elsewhere.

Costello, Peter. *The Magic Zoo: The Natural History of Fabulous Animals.* New York: St. Martin's Press, 1979.
Costello's bestiary, which focuses on about twenty creatures, including the unicorn, the mermaid, and the dragon, discusses the sources and real-life counterparts of these various legends. Illustrated and with extensive bibliographies.

Dove, Dr. W. Franklin. "Artificial Production of the Fabulous Unicorn: A Modern Interpretation of an Ancient Myth." *The Scientific Monthly* 42:431–436; May, 1936.
How Dr. Dove made his unicorn, as well as some musings on the history and character of the animal.

Freeman, Margaret B. *The Unicorn Tapestries.* New York: The Metropolitan Museum of Art, 1976.
An excellent account of the unicorn in ancient and medieval literature and art—and a detailed, exhaustive discussion of the tapestries. Beautifully illustrated, the book includes many details of the tapestries.

Jung, C. G. *Psychology and Alchemy.* Princeton: Princeton University Press, 1953.
Jung's approaches include the historical and the symbolic, and he discusses Indian and Persian legends often not considered in other sources.

Ley, Willy. *The Lungfish, the Dodo and the Unicorn: An Excursion into Romantic Zoology.* New York: The Viking Press, 1948.
The historical discussion of the unicorn in this book begins with Pliny and ends with Dr. Dove. One of the basics.

Lum, Peter. *Fabulous Beasts.* New York: Pantheon, 1951.
An excellent introduction to the subject of imaginary animals, this book has a well-researched chapter on the unicorn that includes historical background and interpretation.

Poltarnees, Welleran. *A Book of Unicorns.* La Jolla: Green Tiger Press, 1978.
A collection of art work and quotations from such historical figures as Ctesias and Isidore of Seville.

Rowland, Beryl. *Animals with Human Faces: A Guide to Animal Symbolism.* Knoxville: The University of Tennessee Press, 1973.
A fascinating and scholarly book which draws on primary sources to provide an analysis of why certain qualities became associated with certain animals. Attractively illustrated and designed, this bestiary considers fifty-seven creatures ranging from the amphisbaena to the wolf.

Shepard, Odell. *The Lore of the Unicorn.* 1930. Reprint. New York: Harper and Row, 1979 (paperback).
This is the classic book about the unicorn. Written in an intelligent and engaging manner, it explores the lore and history of the unicorn in spectacular detail and with a muted humor. Even the footnotes make good reading.

Topsell, Edward. *The Elizabethan Zoo: A Book of Beasts Both Fabulous And Authentic.* Boston: David R. Godine, Publisher, 1979.
This book is an abridged version of an actual Elizabethan bestiary first published in 1658.

Vietmeyer, Noel D., "Rare Narwhal Inspired the Myth of the Unicorn," *Smithsonian.* 10: 118–123; Feb., 1980.
Discusses the discovery of the narwhal and the use of its horn and provides some information about the narwhal today.

White, T. H. *The Bestiary: A Book of Beasts.* New York: G. P. Putnam's Sons, 1953.
A translation from a Latin bestiary of the twelfth century, this book is full of strange beliefs about the habits of animals, both real and imaginary, and it gives Christian interpretations of the import of those habits. It is every bit as deft as we might expect from the author of *The Once and Future King*—a book in which the unicorn also plays a part.

Illustrations and Sources

Fourteenth-century miniature illustrating the traditional enmity between the unicorn and the elephant.

1: Detail from left wing of altarpiece by Hieronymus Bosch (1460–1516). Museo del Prado, Madrid.

2: Detail from *The Garden of Delights,* central panel of altarpiece by Hieronymus Bosch. Museo del Prado, Madrid.

3: Family crests, Great Britain and Ireland. New York Public Library Picture Collection.

5: *Battle of Alexander and the Dragon.* Leaf from *Shah Namah.* Iran, fourteenth century. Ross Collection, Museum of Fine Arts, Boston.

6–7: Twelfth-century miniature from a *Physiologus* manuscript. Courtesy of the Trustees of the British Museum, London.

8–9: Dianne O'Quinn Burke © 1980.

10: Farbenfotografie, Reinhold, Leipzig-Molkar.

11: New York Public Library Picture Collection.

12: Ms. fr. 1061, fol. 155, Musée Condé, Chantilly.

13 top: Kunsthistorisches Museum, © Photo Meyer, Wien.

13 bottom: New York Public Library Picture Collection.

14: Bayerisches Nationalmuseum, Munich.

15: Public Library, Rouen, from the New York Public Library Picture Collection.

16: Fonds Strozzi, Ms. 174, fol. 28B, Biblioteca Laurenziana, Florence.

17 top: Landesmuseum, Zurich.

17 bottom: New York Public Library Picture Collection.

18–19: The Samuel H. Kress Collection, The National Museum of Art, Washington, D.C.

20; 21 top: The Museum of Fine Arts, Boston.

21 bottom: Ms. Douce 366, fol. 55^v, Bodleian Library, Oxford.

22: Chruch of Our Lady, Memmingen, Bavaria.

23 top: Museum of Fine Arts, Boston.

23 bottom: Co. facs. 4° 132b–1, Wurttemburgische Landesbibliothek, Stuttgart.

24–25: Mittelrheinisches Landesmuseum, Mainz.

28: Add. Ms. 47682, f. 2v. Courtesy of the Trustees of the British Museum, London.

29: New York Public Library Picture Collection.

30 top: *Illustratus Medicinialis,* Ulm, 1663.

30 bottom; 31: Gerona Cathedral, MAS, Barcelona.

32–33: The Vatican. Editorial Photocolor Archives, Inc., New York.

34 top: Gerona Cathedral, MAS, Barcelona.

34 bottom: Ms. 251, fol. 16. Reproduced by permission of the Syndics of the Fitzwilliam Museum, Cambridge, England.

35: Library of Holy Cross College, Vallodolid. MAS, Barcelona.

36 left: Add. Ms. 38.122, fol. 12. Courtesy of the Trustees of the British Museum.

36–37: Woodcut in *Neue Kwistliche Figuren Biblischer Historien*, Basel, 1576.

37: After the *Carta Marina* of Bishop Olaus Magnus, Venice, 1539.

39: Royal Ms. 2B vii, fol. 6v. Courtesy of the Trustees of the British Museum.

40: No. 19.174, Courtesy of the Smithsonian Institution, Freer Gallery of Art, Washington, D.C.

41; 42–43: Courtesy of the Kirin Brewery Company, Ltd., Tokyo.

44: Old pen drawing.

45: Courtesy of The Francis E. Fowler, Jr. Foundation Museum, Beverly Hills, California.

46: Photo by Akira Kumagai. Courtesy of the Kirin Brewery Company, Ltd., Tokyo.

47: No. 48.17, Courtesy of the Smithsonian Institution, Freer Gallery of Art, Washington, D.C.

48–49: Old pen drawing.

50; 51: Photos by Akira Kumagai. Courtesy of the Kirin Brewery Company, Ltd., Tokyo.

52: Courtesy of the Pierpont Morgan Library, New York.

53: Drawing after a manuscript in the British Museum, London.

54 top: Courtesy of the Smithsonian Institution, Freer Gallery of Art, Washington, D.C.

54 bottom: Staatliche Museum, Berlin.

55: 10.593 f. 188, Walters Art Gallery, Baltimore.

57: No. 38.2, Courtesy of the Smithsonian Institution, Freer Gallery of Art, Washington, D.C.

58: 4040 Latin 8501, fº 34rº, Bibliothèque Nationale, Paris.

59: 3239 Latin 8501, fol. 51, Bibliothèque Nationale, Paris.

60: No. 07.625, Courtesy of the Smithsonian Institution, Freer Gallery of Art, Washington, D.C.

61: Robert Garrett Collection, No. 82G, Princeton University Library.

62: The Cleveland Museum of Art, Purchased from the J. H. Wade Fund.

64: Courtesy of the Smithsonian Institution, Freer Gallery of Art, Washington, D.C.

65: New York Public Library Picture Collection.

66–67: *Theatrum universale omnium animalium*, Heilbronn, 1755.

69: Courtesy of The Francis E. Fowler, Jr. Foundation Museum, Beverly Hills, California.

70–71: Rietberg Museum, Zurich.

73: Photo from Prentenkabinet R.U., Leyden.

76: The Cloisters Collection of the Metropolitan Museum of Art, New York. Gift of John D. Rockefeller, Jr., 1937.

77: New York Public Library Picture Collection.

78–85: The Cloisters Collection of the Metropolitan Museum of Art, New York. Gift of John D. Rockefeller, Jr., 1937.

86: Courtesy of the Pierpont Morgan Library, New York.

88: Cluny Museum, Paris.

89: New York Public Library Picture Collection.

90–91; 92–93: Cluny Museum, Paris.

94–95: The Cleveland Museum of Art, The Coralie Walter Hanna Memorial Collection, Gift of Leonard C. Hanna, Jr.

96 left: Cluny Museum, Paris.

96 right: The National Gallery of Art, Washington, D.C.

97: Designed by A. G. Law Samson, heraldic writer to the Lyon Court, H. M. Register House, Edinburgh. From *Scots Heraldry* by Sir Thomas Innes of Learney. Oliver and Boyd, Edinburgh.

98–99: New York Public Library Picture Collection.

100: Historisches Museum, Basel.

101: New York Public Library Picture Collection.

102: Photo from Copperplate Engravings Collection of the Public Art Collection, Basel.

103 top: Rijksmuseum, Amsterdam.

103 bottom: Ms. laur. Med. Pala. 143, Biblioteca Laurenzia, Florence.

104–105: Museum of Fine Arts, Boston.

106–107: Courtesy of the Trustees of the British Museum, London.

108–109: Courtesy of the Trustees of the British Museum, London.

109: Samuel H. Kress Collection, National Gallery of Art, Washington, D.C.

112: Galleria Borghese, Rome. SCALA/New York, Florence. Photo courtesy of Editorial Photocolor Archives, New York.

113: New York Public Library Picture Collection.

114: Cod. cl. 11, N. 132, fol. 233v, Biblioteca Estense, Modena.

115: Bodleian Library, Oxford.

116 top: *Hortus Sanitatis*, Mainz, 1491.

116 bottom: Agustin Durán y Sanpere's volume on Spain in *Populare Druck graphik Europas*, Munich, 1971.

117: Rijksmuseum, Amsterdam.

118: P.H.M. 3704, Germanisches Nationalmuseum, Nürnberg.

119: Christian Museum, Eztergom, Hungary. Courtesy Marcel Schurman Co., Inc., San Francisco.

120–121: Paintings by Susan Boulet, Oakland, California.

123: Agustine Museum, Freiburg (Breisgau). Photo from Karl Albert Publications, Bildverlag, Freiburg in Breisgau.

126: Ms. fr. 9140, fol. 323, Bibliothèque Nationale, Paris.

127: New York Public Library Picture Collection.

128: Harl. 4751, f. 15, 50418, British Museum, London.

129: New York Public Library Picture Collection.

130 top: Ulysses Aldrovardi, *Monstrorum historiae*, 1642.

130 bottom: Ms. fr. 2810, fol. 85, Bibliothèque Nationale, Paris.

131: Peter Pomet, *Histoire des Drogues*, Paris, 1694.

132–133: Bibliothèque Nationale, Paris.

134: Erhard Renwick, *Perigrinationes ad Terram Sanctum*, 1486.

135: Ms. fr. 9140, fol. 323, Bibliothèque Nationale, Paris.

136 top: Berne *Physiologus*, ninth century.

136 middle: Engraving by J. Collaert after J. ven der Staet.

136 bottom: Woodcut by Johann Zainer, from *Aesop's Fables*, Ulm, ca. 1476.

Hearing *from* The Lady with the Unicorn *series made about 1500.*

146; 147; 148: Dove, Dr. William Franklin, *Scientific Monthly*, New York, May, 1936.
149: Kunsthistorisches Museum © Photo Meyer, Wien.
150: Gustave Moreau Museum, Paris.
151: Jean Cocteau drawing for *The Lady with the Unicorn* ballet, presented originally in Munich, 1953. From the estate of Heinz Rosen.
152–153: Cluny Museum, Paris.
154–155: L. Leslie Brooke, *Ring o' Roses*, London: Frederick Warne & Co. Ltd., 1922.
156: James Endicott © 1980, courtesy of Portal Publications, Corte Madera, California.
157: Michael von Meyer, courtesy of Portal Publications.
158: Jacquelyn Sage, from *In Pursuit of the Unicorn*, Pomegranate Artbooks, Corte Madera, California, 1980.
159: Kirwan, from *In Pursuit of the Unicorn*, Op. cit.
160–161: The Bliss Collection, Metropolitan Museum of Art, New York.
162–163: The Cloisters Collection of the Metropolitan Museum of Art, New York. Gift of John D. Rockefeller, Jr., 1937.
164: Christalene Loren, Topanga, California.
165: Courtesy of Kirin Brewery Company, Ltd., Tokyo.
166 top: NAL, *Omni* magazine, October 1978.
166 bottom: Laurie Noble, © 1979.
167 top: James Thurber © 1940, Helen Thurber © 1968, from *Fables for Our Time*, Harper and Row, New York. Originally printed in *The New Yorker*.
167 bottom: Schmidt Lithograph Co., courtesy of the Gold Buckle Association, © Portal Publications, Corte Madera, California.
168 top: Jonathan Meader © 1979, from *In Pursuit of the Unicorn*, Pomegranate Artbooks, Corte Madera, California.
168 bottom: June Sobel © 1979.
169: The Whaling Museum, New Bedford, Mass.
170: Susan Boulet, from *In Pursuit of the Unicorn*, Pomegranate Artbooks.
171: Susan Boulet, Oakland, California.
172–173: Dianne Burke, 1980, Los Angeles, California.
175: Susan Boulet, from *In Pursuit of the Unicorn*, Pomegranate Artbooks.
176–177: Susan Boulet.
178; 181; 183; 184–185: Dianne Burke.
186: Illustration from a fourteenth-century Persian manuscript. I. 6943 fol. 262v. Islamisches Museum, Staatliche Museen, Berlin/DDR.
188: Detail from Royal Ms. 2B VII, fol. 100v. Courtesy of the Trustees of the British Museum.
190: *Hearing* from *The Lady with the Unicorn* tapestries. Cluny Museum, Paris.
191: *A Mon Seul Desir*, the final tapestry in *The Lady with the Unicorn* series. Cluny Museum, Paris.
192: Publisher's House Seal, 1908, by Melchior Lechter (1865–1937).

137 top: Abraham Lambsprincke, *Musaeum Hermeticum*, 1625.
137 bottom: Thomas Bartholinus, *De Unicornu*, second edition.
138–139: Ms. fr. 2810, fol. 59, Bibliothèque Nationale, Paris.
140: Museo del Prado, Madrid.
141: New York Public Library Picture Collection.
142: Peter Pomet, *Histoire des Drogues*, Paris, 1694.
143: Church of St. Martin at Zillis in the Grisons, photo by Boissonas, Geneva.
144–145: Museo del Prado, Madrid.

A Mon Seul Desir, *the final tapestry in* The Lady with the Unicorn *series made about 1500.*